"Doing School"

"Doing School"

How We Are Creating a Generation of Stressed

Out, Materialistic, and Miseducated Students

DENISE CLARK POPE

YALE UNIVERSITY PRESS / NEW HAVEN AND LONDON

Designed by Rebecca Gibb.
Set in Minion type by Integrated Publishing Solutions, Grand Rapids, Michigan.
Printed in the United States of America.

Library of Congress Cataloging-in-Publication Data
Pope, Denise Clark, 1966–
"Doing school" : how we are creating a generation of stressed out,
materialistic, and miseducated students / Denise Clark Pope.
p. cm.
Includes bibliographical references.
ISBN 0-300-09013-7 (alk. paper)
1. High school students—United States.   2. Academic achievement—United States.
3. Student aspirations—United States.   I. Title.

LA229 .P59 2001
373.18—dc21
2001026139
The paper in this book meets the guidelines for permanence and durability of
the Committee on Production Guidelines for Book Longevity of the Council
on Library Resources.

10 9 8 7 6 5 4 3 2 1

To Kevin, Eve, Teresa, Michelle, and Roberto
and
To Buddy Peshkin,
who will always hold a special place in my memory

Contents

Preface

Ignorance about adolescents leads us to trivialize their experience
—*Penelope Eckert,* Jocks and Burnouts

In tenth grade I fell in love with Walt Whitman. I went home and declared my adoration for the man and his work, adding that I had most certainly found my calling in life. Never before had I met someone whose words were so invigorating and whose poetry inspired me to try to write my own. I remember reading and rereading *Leaves of Grass* on the front lawn of my high school, attempting to crack the hidden code of the language, to discover meaning behind the words. I remember the excitement of coming to understand a difficult term or phrase, and of being in awe of a talent that could invoke such passionate feelings within me.

My memories of high school in the early 1980s abound with such moments of passion and engagement. Though I experienced my strongest feelings in English class, marveling at the artistry of Shake-speare, Faulkner, Emerson, and Dickinson, I also remember enjoy-ing subjects in my science and history courses. I spent hours with friends pondering existential issues that emerged from our studies, such as the limits of free will and the origins of life. I remember how earnest we were in these conversations, and though we called our-selves "geeks" (a label we were given by other students in the school) for being engrossed by such ideas, it seemed clear that our high school experiences played a significant role in helping to shape us as thinking, feeling, human beings. We had learned to love learn-ing and the excitement that accompanied it.

Years later, as a high school English teacher, I often reflected on these school experiences and attempted to foster this same kind of excitement in my own students. I wanted to spark a love for liter-ature, a commitment to writing and speaking with passion and verve, and a desire to read and write as a way of understanding hu-manity and of exploring the world. During the brief 50 minutes I saw my students each day, I couldn't help but wonder if any felt the way that I had in high school. Some appeared well-prepared and eager to learn; some reluctantly participated in the lessons; and others refused to take part at all, seeming to ignore me and neglect the daily assignments. Though I believed I had concrete evidence of student learning (or lack thereof), in the form of essays, quizzes, homework assignments, and class participation, I felt that I still did not know the level of student engagement with the material. I rea-soned that I could not determine this unless I spoke with the stu-dents themselves. I wanted to find out what was going on inside their heads as they sat in my classroom each day. What did they make of their school experiences? Which educational endeavors, if any, were meaningful and valuable to them? Since they spent seven hours, five days a week, confined within the walls of the public high school, what did they believe were the deep consequences of their compulsory attendance at the school?

As I reviewed the literature on adolescents and secondary schools, I noticed a peculiar gap in the research in this area. I found a wide range of studies on adolescent behavior in schools, studies that addressed academic achievement, study habits, classroom discipline, peer culture, and youth dropout rates.[1] However, I did not find many studies that addressed the educational experience in school from the adolescents' points of view. The few studies I found that relied on the youth's perspectives examined mostly the social aspects of schooling, such as life in the hallways and parking lots, instead of the students' classroom experiences and the character of their intellectual engagement—topics that lie at the very heart of the mission of the school.[2] It seems ironic that we require young people to attend high school, and yet we know relatively little about what they think of the place.

One reason we do not hear much about students' curricular experiences may be that we have not asked them specifically to reflect on these experiences.[3] Attempting to hear the youths' perspectives seems vital if we are to achieve a sense of community in our schools and if we aspire to create conditions conducive to student growth. John Dewey (1938) urged educators to have a "sympathetic understanding of individuals as individuals [in order to have an] idea of what is actually going on in the minds of those who are learning" (p. 39). He encouraged taking the time to get to know students, to seek their opinions and interests, and to listen to their stories in order to foster educational experiences that aroused curiosity and strengthened initiative. When an average high school teacher might have more than 160 students, arriving at this kind of understanding is no easy task. By focusing on a few adolescents for more than eight months, I attempt in this research to get to know students as individuals, to help convey their experiences and their perspectives in order to help achieve the kind of understanding Dewey advocated.

About the study: I chose to do this research in a high school with a reputation for caring teachers, innovative programs, and strong leadership. It is a comprehensive school with a diverse population where approximately 95 percent of the school's graduates attend college.[4] I asked for a range of students, diverse in gender, ethnicity, socioeconomic background, and academic interests in the tenth and eleventh grades whom the administrators considered to be "successful." I allowed school officials to define the nature of the students' success. Five students were then selected based on multiple recommendations from teachers, counselors, and administrators.

Over the course of a school semester, I shadowed each of these students, closely observing their behavior in classrooms, accompanying them to all school-related events, talking with them at length during the school day, and interviewing them each week to help them reflect on their experiences. I also used student journals, essays, and class notes when appropriate to discern the students' perspectives on the curriculum.[5] In order to achieve a sense of trust and rapport with the students, I limited my data collection to focus on the adolescents. I did not interview teachers, parents, or administrators. Hence, the experiences captured here are rooted in the words and actions of the students themselves. In each case, the youth played critical roles in helping to shape the nature and form of the portraits that follow.

Acknowledgments

Throughout the process of researching and writing this book, I have had the invaluable support of several individuals. I am especially grateful to Stanford professors Elliot Eisner, Buddy Peshkin, and Ray McDermott, who offered sage advice and guidance. Elliot encouraged me to pursue the topic of educational experience and helped me to think critically about the high school curriculum and its effect on students. He challenged me throughout the process to examine the larger consequences of my research and to write for a broad audience. I thank him for all his help on this project and for serving as my advisor and mentor.

Buddy, too, served as a valuable advisor and friend. During our frequent phone calls and meetings, he graciously shared his knowledge of qualitative methodology and helped guide me through the day-to-day process of data collection, analysis, and writing. I was fortunate to know and work closely with Buddy on this book and other projects until his death in December 2000. I am grateful for his wisdom and understanding and know that I am a better researcher because of him.

I thank Ray for his help in shaping the study and for his vast knowledge of relevant literature. He reminded me of the importance of educational context and of the researcher's limitations in capturing students' experiences. In addition, Mike Atkin kindly served as an "outside reader" for an early draft and offered useful suggestions and encouragement.

I am also grateful to Sam Intrator, Lissa Soep, Susan Verducci, Liz Lazaroff, and Nicole Holthius for offering constructive criticism and practical advice. In addition to being supportive friends and colleagues, they served as role models who helped me to believe it was possible to conduct a study of this nature while balancing work and family life. Nel Noddings, Mark Batenburg, Don Hill, and Michael Newman as well as my editors, Susan Arellano and Margaret Otzel, each read full drafts of the manuscript and offered valuable critiques. And I am particularly indebted to Simone Schweber and Kathy Simon, my writing group members, who read early chapters with care, edited rough drafts, and provided keen insights and analysis. Their friendship, intellect, generosity, and enthusiasm were indispensable in helping me to complete this project.

I also wish to thank my family members for their ongoing support and encouragement. My parents provided assistance in a variety of ways, serving as cheerleaders, critics, and "emergency" babysitters. They fostered in me a love of learning and a desire to study the field of education. In addition, I want to thank my daughters, Megan and Allison, both of whom were born in the midst of the research process, for their patience and understanding when "mommy went off to work." And I am eternally grateful for the love and support of my husband, Mike, who patiently listened to my questions and concerns day after day, read multiple versions of all of my chapters, and offered invaluable help.

Finally, I could not have done this work without five special high school students who let me in to their lives and told me the stories of their school experiences. As busy as they were, they welcomed me each morning and made the research experience an enjoyable one as I shadowed them from class to class. I dedicate this book to them and hope that their portraits inspire other students and educators to make significant changes to improve the quality of secondary education.

CHAPTER 1

Welcome to Faircrest High

Faircrest High School's values: Be punctual, prepared, tolerant, honest, respectful, responsible.
—posted on a sign in a FHS classroom

"I wish I could have a class full of students like Eve,"[1] says the chair of the history department, describing one of his "ideal" pupils. Eve has a 3.97 grade point average. She is ranked in the top 10 percent of her class and is enrolled in every honors and advanced placement level course available to her. Her résumé lists more than 25 school activities in which she has participated since her freshman year, ranging from field hockey and symphonic band to student council, Spanish club, and Junior Statesmen of America.

Another teacher recommends Kevin. He is well known at the school because of his friendly personality, his high grades, and his star performance on the school soccer team. For the past two years he has led a student-run community service project that delivers school supplies and clothing to less privileged children in neighboring towns. He takes classes from both the college preparatory track as well as the honors track, and he is in the highest possible courses for his grade level in three subject areas: English, history, and French. "He is so smart and such a nice boy," says the PE teacher, "if I had a son, I would want one like him."

Other names come up multiple times. Michelle, an exceptional drama and music student, is recommended for her acting performances, her top grades, and her enrollment in a special program called The Community Project. Teresa is an outstanding student in the new business theme house, excelling in business computing skills. She impresses teachers by her desire to "challenge" herself and her commitment to the Mexican Student Association. Finally, there is Roberto, who hopes to be the first in his immediate family to attend college. He is recommended for his diligence and dedication to this goal, as well as his successful record in a seminar course in which he was awarded the Coordinator's Commendation for Excellence.

"These students represent some of our best and brightest," a guidance counselor notes with pride. "They are good kids who work hard and do well. Actually, I could name many others just like them, but you only need five." Such was my introduction to Faircrest High.

I chose to study students at Faircrest because of its excellent reputation. The school, located in a wealthy California suburb, has one of the lowest dropout rates in the state, small class sizes, and a "long-standing tradition of hiring the best teachers to provide the highest quality instruction."[2] The school's annual report lists college acceptance rates, scholastic aptitude test results, and the number of students commended for National Merit distinction, all of which rank Faircrest well above the state average. More than one-third of the student body is enrolled in honors and advanced placement (AP) courses, and many of these students "get accepted to universities such as Stanford, Harvard, [and] Yale."

Evidence of student success is everywhere. Teachers announce awards over the loudspeaker each morning: "Congratulations to Mr. Parker's class and the three winners of the state math competition ... [names are read aloud]. Overall, Faircrest came in second, just behind Alpine School this year. Let's come in first next time!" The school sends dozens of letters home congratulating students who maintain 4.0 averages each semester. Teachers post the best essays and test results on classroom walls, hanging banners with the names of students who earned perfect scores on advanced placement exams from the past ten years. And each month, every department honors an outstanding student, posting his or her photo on a central bulletin board and listing the names in the yearbook. In publications, on the walls, and over the loudspeakers, Faircrest's top students are impressive. They are articulate, focused, multitalented, and industrious. They are the pride of the public education system and the hope for the future.

Listen to the students, though, and you'll hear a different side of success. To keep up her grades, Eve sleeps just two to three hours each night and lives in a constant state of stress. Kevin faces anxiety and frustration as he attempts to balance the high expectations of his father with his own desire to "have a life" outside of school. Michelle struggles to find a way to pursue her love for drama without compromising her college prospects. And both Teresa and Roberto resort to drastic actions when they worry that they will not maintain the grades they need for future careers. All of them admit to doing things that they're not proud of in order to succeed in school.

These students explain that they are busy at what they call "doing school." They realize that they are caught in a system where achievement depends more on "doing"—going through the correct motions—than on learning and engaging with the curriculum. Instead of thinking deeply about the content of their courses and delving into projects and assignments, the students focus on managing the work load and honing strategies that will help them to achieve high grades. They learn to raise their hands even when they don't know the answers to the teachers' questions in order to appear interested. They understand the importance of forming alliances and classroom treaties to win favors from teachers and administrators. Some feel compelled to cheat and to contest certain grades and decisions in order to get the scores they believe they need for the future. As Kevin asserts:

> People don't go to school to learn. They go to get good grades which brings them to college, which brings them the high-paying job, which brings them to happiness, so they think. But basically, grades is where it's at.

Values normally espoused in schools, such as honesty, diligence, and teamwork, necessarily come into question when the students must choose between these ideals and getting top grades. It is hard to be a team player when you are competing with peers for an A grade on the class curve. It is difficult to remain honest when so much in school depends on appearing alert and prepared, and when there is too much work to do and too little time in which to do it. The workload is so great and the expectations so high that these students feel obligated to give up recreation and sleep time as well as many aspects of a social life in order to succeed. Eve explains: "All year I sat and stared at the names on the banner in my history class, and it became my entire goal; . . . I swore I would get my name up there if it killed me." Her devotion to success eventually earns her a spot on the history advanced placement banner. And though the pressure to succeed does not "kill" her, it does make her physically ill. She, like the others, has learned to do "whatever it takes" to get ahead, even if this means sacrificing "individuality, health, and happiness"—not to mention compromising ethical principles.

These students regret the frenetic pace of their school days and the undue stress they endure. They do not like manipulating the system or compromising their beliefs and values by kissing up, lying, and cheating. But they also do not like what they see as the alternative. They believe job prospects and income are better for college graduates, especially for those who earn credentials from prestigious universities.[3] Lower grades and test scores might jeopardize future wealth and well-being. Hence, the students are victims of what I call the "grade trap." They feel bound by a narrow definition of success and resigned to a system in which ultimate satisfaction may not be attainable.

To their teachers, administrators, parents, and community, these students represent the "ideal." They are motivated to get ahead and work hard to achieve high grades. They participate in extracurricular activities, serve their communities, earn numerous awards and honors, and appear to uphold the values posted on the walls of the Faircrest classrooms. This book examines the behavior behind the success. The chapters, written as individual portraits, offer an inside view of the complexity of student life as well as the persistent dilemmas faced by everyone in the school system.

Although Faircrest High, along with most schools, claims to value certain character traits such as honesty and respect, the student experiences in the competitive academic environment reflect the conflicting goals inherent in the educational system today.[4] As you read about the students—whose stories may resonate with "successful" high school students throughout this country—ask yourself the following questions: What kind of behavior is fostered by the expectations of the school community and by those outside of the school? Can students meet these expectations without sacrificing personal and academic goals and beliefs? Can parents encourage their children to strive for future success without pushing too hard or advocating questionable behavior? What can school teachers and administrators do in light of the constraints of college admission requirements and national education policies that spur competition for high grades and test scores? Are we fostering an environment that promotes intellectual curiosity, cooperation, and integrity, or are our schools breeding anxiety, deception, and frustration? Are they impeding the very values they claim to embrace? Are we preparing students well for the future? Are they ready for the world of work? Are they ready to be valuable members of our society? And is this the kind of education to which we as a nation should aspire?

Listen to the voices of these five students.

CHAPTER 2

Kevin Romoni:
A 3.8 Kind of Guy

I've been really fortunate, and I mean the breaks went my way. You know, I didn't let up and I tried almost as hard as I could, and it's just that I don't want to let other people down. . . . I don't know if you'd say I'm like a people pleaser. I only do stuff to please other people because pleasing other people pleases me.

Kevin Romoni *is* a people pleaser. He's the student who offers to collect the homework for the teacher, or to gather the PE equipment. He says, "Bonjour, Madame" each morning to his French teacher and asks about her weekend. He is the class cheerleader, the one who gives the high five to students when they answer questions correctly. He pats a nearby shoulder and says, "Good job, Jerome. You're a star." He reminds his fellow English students to clap loudly during the oral presentations—"because it takes guts to get up there, dudes." He is also happy to play the clown at times, cracking a joke to break the tension in history class before a test or attempting to tell a funny story with his poor accent in French class about president "Beeeeel Cleenton and Madame Hillary." He is short for his age, with straight brown hair that hangs in his face according to the latest style, and a dazzling smile. A natural athlete, he is the most valuable player on the junior varsity soccer team and was picked for all-league this year. He is also considered to be a good student and regularly gets his name on the school bulletin board under the heading "students with honors." He is bright, funny, polite, and charming. And he knows it.

He describes himself in his writing as a "glass is half-full kind of guy," and he certainly has reason to feel this way. His family moved from a large city to the suburbs when Kevin was in the third grade. They live in a newly remodeled home on a beautiful tree-lined street in one of the best areas of town. Kevin has his own room, complete with a large-screen television set and all the newest video games, a jumbo stereo system, Macintosh computer and printer, and several photographs of past prom dates and best friends. He points out many times to me that he has had the same close-knit group of friends since he moved to this community, and they hang out together every day. They go off campus to lunch, play basketball, listen to the newest CDs and take most of their classes together.

His parents are educated Faircrest professionals. His father, a Caucasian, is an aeronautical engineer who holds degrees from Stanford, Berkeley, and the University of California at San Diego, and his mother, a first-generation Japanese-American, put herself through night school and became an executive assistant to the CEO of one of the largest consulting firms in the area. Kevin has an older sister who dropped out a couple of times from community college and, as he describes it, "really messed up her life." He also has a sister, eleven months younger, who attends the same high school but

is in a lower academic track than Kevin and has separate friends
and interests.

His younger sister doesn't receive the kind of high grades that
Kevin does, but he characterizes her as a better student because she
"studies her butt off, makes index cards, and does everything a
good student is supposed to do." He, on the other hand, describes
himself as a different kind of student:

> I would say I am a good person, not a good student. . . . I mean,
> I'm not one of those people that shoots for a B. I'll do what it
> takes to get an A, but I don't think I'm a good student. I mean, I
> don't study as often as I should, I don't read as often as I should,
> I don't keep up as often as I should. I'm still getting by, getting
> mostly A's, but it's just by the skin of my teeth . . . and I really
> want to change that. I mean my parents say it's going to catch up
> with me, catch up with me really quick. It's going to have bad
> effects, . . . that's what they always say.

Kevin feels pressure to change his study habits, even though he admits that he is doing well in school. He strives to meet the expectations of his parents and teachers—to be the good student—and he
worries about letting them down.

In fact, the pressure to please others is so intense for Kevin that
it dominates his school experience. Instead of engaging with his
classes, he spends most of his time trying to obtain the "good
grades" that will get him into college and thus make his parents
happy. He's aware of the stress he feels and reluctantly tells me that
it's "probably beneficial," believing that without it, he wouldn't be
where he is today. The irony is not apparent to Kevin, though, that
perhaps without the undue pressure, he might have quite a different school experience, one not so heavily marked by competition,
frustration, and fear.

Pleasing Dad: The "Good" Student

KEVIN
ROMONI

Kevin's father told him once that "pressure turns coal into dia-
monds," and, as is clear from many of our conversations, Kevin
feels pressure:

> I can't look like I am slacking off. This is very important, *very*.
> More important to my dad than to me, but also important for
> me. I have taken seven periods [the normal load is six] my whole
> career here, so I don't want to look like a slacker.
>
> See, my older sister really messed up her life. When we moved,
> you know, from Redland, she got caught in that whole transfer
> thing. She was a sophomore then—my age now—and had a
> really tough time adjusting to a new school. She graduated in,
> like, 1988, then went to community college—dropped out, went
> back and forth. Then she dropped out finally. . . . She did get A
> plusses though in French like every year. She's basically fluent.
>
> That's why I took French, because my mom and sisters took it.
> That's why I want to do well in school. To prove to my dad and to
> justify the move was good. It is important for me to do well. . . .
> See my parents want me to do this engineer or lawyer thing. . . .
> My dad wants me to go to Stanford like him. He says college leads
> to success.

Don't look like a slacker. Don't be like your sister. Go to college and
be a success. Make us proud. Kevin explains that he hears over and
over again about the importance of getting good grades for mainly
external, future-oriented benefits—college acceptance, his parents'
pride, a lucrative career. Rarely does he hear that he should strive to
do well in school for his own edification and enjoyment. Whether

or not his parents intended the messages to be heard this way, this is how Kevin characterizes them.

It is no wonder then that Kevin is obsessed with his grades. He calculates his grade point average (GPA) several times a day—whenever he gets back a test or quiz. He asks his counselor for advice as to which courses will "look better" on his transcript for college: For instance, he can take French IV, where he might get a B, or start a new language in his junior year where he has a likely chance of getting an A, since it will be an introductory level course. His counselor says the best option is for him get an A in French, but if that is not possible, then his next best option is to take Latin I. Kevin opts for the latter, explaining that Latin might help him with the vocabulary section of his SATs. He also admits that he takes physical education every year because it's an "easy A to pad the GPA," and he is thankful that the University of California system awards extra points on the transcripts of students who take advanced placement and honors classes. On the rare occasion that he gets a C, "a practically failing grade" by his standards, he re-takes the class during the summer to replace the grade on his transcript. He did this with his French class last year and "will probably need to do it again." Unfortunately, he is not allowed to re-take his English course, and therefore becomes extremely upset when he learns that he might get a B+ for the semester. In every school decision he makes, the paramount importance of grades is clear:

> My goal is to get a 3.7 or higher. . . . My dad will give me 50 bucks if I get it—even though 50 bucks isn't really that much. . . . Do I have any other goals? [long pause] I mean look, grades are the focus. I tell you, people don't go to school to learn. They go to get good grades which brings them to college, which brings them the high-paying job, which brings them to happiness, so they think. But basically, grades is where it's at. They're the focus

of every student in every high school in every place in America and otherwise. Period.

In the narrow world of the academic track, his assessment appears accurate. Most of his friends seem intent on achieving good grades, and many discuss future college plans with certainty. Aside from the usual high school banter about sex, music, food, and parties, their classroom conversations often turn to grades and the stress of having too much work to do. Though this might not be the norm for "every student in every high school," in Kevin's world, getting high grades is a primary goal.

With this focus clearly in mind, Kevin uses various strategies to achieve his goal: He "kisses up," compromises, begs, and even resorts at times to cheating, in his efforts to be the "good student." He also does the "minimum required to get by"—usually at the last minute.

Kevin believes that he is "the biggest procrastinator known to man." He typically puts off starting his homework until nine or ten o'clock at night and often opts to "wing" things the next day at school if he is not adequately prepared. He waits until the very last moment before starting to write a paper or work on a large project, and this delay usually results in a marathon work session the night before the due date. He proudly tells horror stories of staying up for two straight days writing his English I-search paper (a large research project on the daily practices of the local police) or reading 130 pages of his history text the night before the test. His parents are very concerned about these study habits and even bought him special self-help cassette tapes on procrastination, which, he says with a grin, he "[hasn't] even turned on yet. Talk about procrastination."

He manages to get high grades despite such late starts because he knows the system well. He knows, for example, that his math and

French teachers only glance at the pages when they check in the homework, so he frequently skips some exercises. He also knows KEVIN that he has a real talent for "winging it"—especially on oral pre-ROMONI sentations or class discussions. A few well-placed questions during a class discussion serve to disguise the fact that he is four chapters behind in his reading. And, in his oral presentation of the paper on local police practices, he knew that a good hypothetical scenario involving the police's prejudicial treatment of teenagers would get his friends talking for at least half of the time he was supposed to be presenting his report. Reflecting on this, he explains his usual approach to "doing school": "I'm obviously not working to my fullest potential, . . . but students have a way of coping by only doing the minimum required. Nobody does more than what they have to."

Again, Kevin generalizes about the way all students handle the pressures to succeed. His statement does not seem as accurate to me as the earlier one on the focus of grades (see the student discussed in the next chapter, for instance); nonetheless, it is important to Kevin that he show he is just like every other student in the way he copes with the stress. This may serve to alleviate any guilt he might feel for not fulfilling his potential, and thereby letting his parents down; if "nobody" does more than is required, then surely Kevin cannot be blamed for only doing the minimum.[1]

This minimalist strategy, however, requires that Kevin bolster his approach by making sure he stays in the good graces of his teachers and the school administrators. He admits that he is "excessively nice and polite" to his teachers and befriends them because they grade his papers. It is not clear whether this strategy wins Kevin higher marks, but he feels such behavior certainly doesn't hurt when the grading process can be quite subjective. Many of his teachers tell me that he is "a really good kid" whom they entrust with such special tasks as taking attendance or delivering messages to the office. In turn, Kevin's amiability allows him to get away with certain behaviors in class that would otherwise not be allowed. He has the special privilege of sitting on top of the file cabinet in his history class, or lying in the middle of the floor to take notes in English, or borrowing the teacher's chair at times in chemistry.

His peers mock him for using this strategy and call him the "biggest kiss ass in the country." For instance, Kevin tells a friend that he "begged his way to an A− in chemistry." The friend is surprised that this teacher (who has a tough reputation in the school) was willing to change the quarter grade. His friend looks at me and explains: "Parents and teachers love Kevin because he is just like Eddie Haskell,[2] coming in and helping them with things and saying, like, 'You look great Mrs. B.'" Kevin admits that politeness has its benefits but also says that he genuinely likes most of his teachers and many of the school administrators and that he would "rather be nice to people in general than just be a jerk." Though this may seem contradictory to his false geniality above, I believe Kevin does like his teachers and honestly prefers to treat people with courtesy and respect. It is part of his cheerleader mentality.

Of course, relying on last minute work sessions and charm can only go so far, and at times Kevin is forced to take more drastic actions to achieve his goals. He occasionally "compares answers" on quizzes and tests and often copies homework from his friends. In his chemistry class, he had a regular cheating system worked out with another student to help him do well on some of the tough exams. When the student was absent during the last chapter test of the year before the final, Kevin was forced to do it alone. He got the test back and proudly showed me the high score: 36 out of 40. He smiled:

> Yeah, I needed that. That's a real morale boost for me. [He whips
> out his calculator and quickly calculates his cumulative chem-

istry grade.] Ninety. Not bad. I still have time to get it higher. [He stares at the test.] Yes! I did it. Without Bob too. Not bad, huh? Hey listen to this answer. . . . [He proceeds to show me his answers to the difficult problems at the end of the test. He looks proud and continues to stare at his answers for the first ten minutes of class.]

KEVIN ROMONI

Clearly, Kevin is more proud of the good grade when he achieves it honestly, but he cannot say at the end of the year that he will not resort again to cheating if he finds he needs to; instead he shakes his head in mock sarcasm and says, "Teenagers these days—no sense of morals."

Kevin explains sincerely that, ideally, he wishes he could forget about the grades and just do the work the way *he* wants to do it. He wishes he could write papers the way he would like to see them written, instead of how the teachers want to see them. He says with a sigh, "I wish I could say I'm an individual, and I am not going to sacrifice my individuality for a grade, you know . . . just write for writing's sake." But he feels he cannot do this. Instead, he says, he "compromises his beliefs" about good writing and tries to guess how the teacher wants the essay to be written or the test question to be answered. He gives up his own sense of style[3] and strives to please others. This is, after all, a key part of what one learns in school—how to assimilate, behave according to a certain system, learn to write and think and speak the way you are taught, the way teachers, parents, and community members believe will lead to future success. In this sense, Kevin is doing well; his strategies, for the most part, seem to get him the results he desires (pleasing his teachers and his parents), and school officials consider him a success.

However, throughout the semester, I see glimpses of a vastly different side of Kevin, a side that is revealed when the strategies don't seem to be working well and when he thinks it is safe to let himself go. This is the furious side of Kevin, or, in his terms, his "competitive nature taking over."

Getting Furious: The Competitor

Kevin hides this fierce side of himself well, because it doesn't jibe with his "nice boy" reputation. It comes out in PE class, in an occasional comment when he receives a low grade, and in his conversations with friends. Behind his motivation to please others is a competitor who wants to succeed. Usually, he vents this rage at himself, pushing himself harder to meet expectations; at other times, he directs it outward. Either way, it is a fairly stark contrast to the Kevin the school community usually sees.

Here is Kevin during PE class:

He is on fire. He races through the warm-up exercises, grabs his tennis racket and screams loudly to no one in particular: "Did I mention we are undefeated so far? UNDEFEATED, BABY!" He screams, "Yes! We are the best!" and throws his racket in the air. "Hey, who hasn't lost to us yet?" During the game he taunts his opponents: "What's the score? Me winning: a lot to a little." He laughs demonically when he makes a shot and wiggles his rear end in the air. After the match he is told to do 25 pushups for jumping over the net in victory. (He never does these.) . . . However, when it looks as if he might lose a game due to several of his double fault serves, he screams at his partner who merely offered some helpful advice: "FUCK! Don't coach me buddy!"

Later in the semester, the PE teacher, who is one of Kevin's biggest fans, tells me about an unusual accident in the warm-up room. Apparently Kevin punched three huge holes in the wall with his feet. At first no one confessed; then, after the teacher called security,

Kevin admitted his guilt, apologized for his mistake, and offered
to pay for the repairs. He swears that he had no idea why he did
it; he just didn't know what came over him. He explains that this
was a good time to be "in" with the administration since he simply
walked up to the principal and said, "Hey Dr. G, I'll take care of it.
OK? I'll pay for it, no problem." And that was that. Kevin received
no other punishment besides paying for the damage.[4] The PE
teacher told me later that the usual punishment for such behavior
is suspension.

KEVIN
ROMONI

Another time I saw this kind of behavior from Kevin was in English class. It was a week before the English I-search paper was due,
and the students were told originally that they would have time
to work on their papers in class that day. Instead, the substitute
teacher assigned a short story and a writing assignment. Kevin was
extremely upset about this change of plans and lost his temper in
front of the class:

> Hell no! I am not reading this story. [He throws the story to the
> ground.] Mr. K is so unfair! I am not doing it. I don't care. I am
> having words with Mr. K. Dude, this is due today? Due today?
> What happened to, "Bring all your work with you to class and
> we will give you time to work"? . . . Mr. K is a liar! He said he
> would give us the whole week to work on it. It's a 30-page paper!

Later he tells me angrily that he had many other assignments due
this week and really needed the time in class to work on his paper.
He felt he was rushing through the assignment and was furious because he wasn't given adequate time to do the research.

A month later while waiting to receive the graded English I-
search paper, Kevin is visibly nervous. He bites his nails and says out
loud, "I revel in my B-plussness. . . . I am settling for mediocrity. . . . Screw A's and go for the B+. It sucks." When he gets his

paper back, he curses loudly: "B! God damn it! I just knew it!" Reflecting on his own behavior later that day, Kevin is still quite upset. He calls his teacher "an unfair asshole" and a "bastard." He admits that he is under "severe" pressure and says,

> I have got to take this pressure off myself somehow. I need an A in English and I am going to get a B+. Sometimes I just feel like giving up. I don't care. Oh, I just know I am going to get a B in that class and I don't know what to do.

When faced with the possibility of not achieving the grade point average he and his parents have set as a goal, Kevin panics. At first he tries to convince himself that it doesn't matter. He says aloud that he will settle for mediocrity—that he just doesn't care. But clearly he does care. The possibility of failure worries him enough that he loses the usual control he exerts over his temper and shows a side of himself of which he says he is not proud. I observe that this furious side is typically reserved for safe places before it is unleashed; he shows it in PE class (where this competitive behavior is usually rewarded—hence, the "easy A" he receives), and he shows it to the substitute teacher, someone who is not in a position of power to grade him. Only when he gets the graded paper back does he curse loudly in front of his English teacher, but he would never call him a "bastard" to his face. He even admits to me that he "b.s.'d his way through the paper," and that it didn't deserve an A, but he *needed* the high grade. When Kevin's usual strategies prove ineffective, he literally does not know what else to do. For the final weeks of the semester, he tries desperately not to care about his English grade, especially because he cannot do much about it at this point, but it continues to infuriate him.[5]

Finally, near the end of the year, the pressure catches up with Kevin. He describes what he calls a "breakdown" that occurred when it became clear that he could not meet everyone's expectations for him:

KEVIN
ROMONI

> I had a breakdown on May 2nd. I was feeling frustrated and behind, and I had all these tests and it was like I was being sucked under . . . sucked down. I wasn't doing well in my classes, and I was feeling helpless, and I *don't* like feeling helpless. I was miserable and tired and I didn't know what to do. So I went to my mom and my dad, and I said, "I can't take this. . . . I just can't do it; I cannot do it anymore." And they said, "Don't worry Kevin, just do your best. That's all we expect from you."
>
> And that was a relief. . . . Actually it was refreshing to hear it from them, and I knew I had to just dust myself off and pick myself up, and start getting my act together. . . . It wasn't really a breakdown. I guess more like I just couldn't take it anymore. I know I needed to motivate myself since no one else could do it for me.
>
> So that's why I studied for chemistry. We didn't have homework because he didn't want to grade it, so I got really lazy and behind and didn't understand the chapter. So I took all these notes and did all these problems, see . . . [He shows me the notes.] And I studied for two tests in one night. I took all these notes on two of my French chapters, too. . . . And then the night after that I finished *Siddhartha*. I read 90 pages in one night.
>
> And then I just started knocking down these tests. Everything is starting to click. [He points to his head and smiles.] . . . Basically I am studying, and I never used to really study before. I would do the homework and listen in class, but I wouldn't really study. Now I do practice problems, take notes, other stuff, too, to study. If you study, you do well.

For Kevin, this "breakdown" signifies a way to re-define himself as a student. He is relieved to hear what he believes are new expectations from his parents—that he do the best he can—which sounds much different to him from "Get the good grades you need to be admitted to Stanford." He implies that these new expectations cause him to be self-motivated (as opposed to working hard to please his parents). Now he is "really" studying, that is, taking notes, reading ahead, and behaving according to his definition of a good student, and he finds he is successful on several tests and assignments in the week that follows his breakdown.

This burst of energy and commitment to studying, however, comes at the end of the year for Kevin, in a final push to get his grades up. He isn't reading *Siddhartha* for understanding (in fact, he tells me later, he didn't "get the book or the stupid group test we had on it, . . . it was too deep"), nor, in my opinion, is he engaging with the chemistry or French material in a significant way. In fact, the breakdown doesn't necessarily change his habits as much as it serves to show the intense pressure he feels to succeed. His parents still expect his "best," so do his teachers, and so, it turns out, does he. Kevin doesn't want to settle for less than a 3.7 grade point average, and when it looks as though he may not achieve this, he pushes himself even harder.

Another episode seems significant in exemplifying Kevin's pattern of "getting furious" when faced with failure and then working hard to fulfill expectations. This time he felt the "competitive urge" to push himself to understand the concept of imaginary numbers. He told me that he didn't want people to "think less of his abilities" and that he had to show them—his parents, teachers, friends—that he could succeed.

I was in class thinking about it, and I was so mad, I was get-

ting furious because I wanted to check my work and it was like
all wrong. I was frustrated like hell. I was getting most of the
right numbers, but not the negative signs. I never wanted to understand something so much in math. It was like a personal thing
between the teacher and me. I was so mad and I was asking like
a flurry of questions and nothing she said was making sense.

The turning point was when I asked if you have a negative sign,
does that account for the fact that "i" is present? And she said she
doesn't know if I should think of it that way—that I should understand it for what it is. . . . She said I need to gain confidence.
She was totally condescending. It was like she thought less of my
abilities, and I hate that. . . . All that period I was so mad. And
[my friends] were understanding it and I couldn't do it. See. Usually I don't get frustrated, but this whole concept of imaginary
numbers perplexes me. I learn something one way my whole life,
and now none of those rules apply. God, it's so frustrating.

Afterward, he works hard to learn the concept on his own, without
the teacher's help. He sees her during break and yells out, "Hey I
think I am finally getting these imaginary numbers!" And later, he
proudly shows me the high score he receives on the unit quiz. In
this case, like the burst of energy he displays after the breakdown,
Kevin is determined to push harder to prove that he can do well. He
seems to reserve this determination (and the anger that usually ac-
companies it) as a sort of last resort, to be used only when things
look most bleak and he is in danger of letting others down.

Thus, the moments of "real studying" (by Kevin's definition of
the term) are rare and usually happen when he determines that he
must change his ways or risk failure. However, I notice a few other
times during the semester when Kevin truly seems to be engaged

with the curriculum. These are the times when he is not necessarily motivated by external factors and seems passionate about
accomplishing his tasks.

Motivated by Passion: The Engaged Learner

Three times during the semester I hear Kevin discuss work he has
done of which he is very proud. He has read *Don Quixote* (the
abridged version), he has written a Family Portrait (five short stories with photos about his childhood), and he has successfully led
PenPals, a community service project.[6] He tells me he read *Don
Quixote* to "kill two birds with one stone." The students were assigned to do a book report in English class, and they were learning
about the Renaissance in European history class, so he chose to
"open [his] mind to a new perspective" and read a more challenging book than he normally would have selected. This time he read
slowly—because he had to in order to understand the difficult language used in the text, and because he wanted to "for the enter-
tainment value." In one of our interviews, he jokingly compares
himself to the knight errant who has a perfect vision of his life in
his head and tries really hard to meet that vision, but "sometimes
he doesn't succeed." Kevin emphasizes that "at least the guy always
tries; he tries real hard." This change in attitude seems significant
because, although he was reading for credit in his classes, he went
beyond the minimum requirement in selecting a difficult book,
and he took the time to think about the book in relation to his own
life. He *felt* something when he read about the knight errant, and
though he mocks himself for making the comparison, his statement implies that he connected with the character and perhaps
learned something about himself, specifically, the value of perseverance. He does not talk in this way about other texts or materials
he encountered during the semester.

Even more striking is how Kevin talks about the Family Portrait he wrote for his English class. The students were asked to find five photographs from their past and to write a short story on the memories they had about each picture. The assignment was to coincide with the reading of *A House on Mango Street*, a book about a Mexican girl's recollection of her childhood. Kevin rolled his eyes when he first received the assignment and wrote the portrait "all in one night." In our final interview, though, he said this was the school project of which he was most proud[7] because:

KEVIN
ROMONI

> I got my best writing grade on this. . . . I think I really deserved that grade, like, I didn't get away with anything on this one. 'Cause it was about my family. When you write about something passionate and you write about real love . . . that's when I think, that's when, like, I get decent grades on poetry and stuff like that because it comes from me here. [He points to his heart.]

He then asked if he could read one of the stories aloud to me. It was a memory of a Christmas Day spent at his uncle's house, accompanied by a picture of a young Kevin and his sisters opening presents under a Christmas tree. It was fairly good tenth-grade writing, with lots of concrete details to describe the day and just the right amount of sentiment:[8]

> Nothing could ever pull us away from our precious toys, nothing except my Grandma Helen's cooking. My Grandma Helen was blessed with a heavenly gift. She had the power to make anything taste good. Her cooking was so good that it could make a five-year-old beg for seconds of lima beans. Our Christmas meal was usually unconventional. We had turkey, homemade pizza, kidney beans, hors d'oeuvres, homemade bread, custard, and ice cream pie. I remember sitting down at Christmas dinner feeling

KEVIN
ROMONI

so important to mingle among the adults for a change. . . . It is strange to think back to those lost Christmases of yesterday. Now my Grandma Helen is gone and the food doesn't taste quite as good. My Uncle Leo is gone and the jokes aren't quite as funny. Christmas gets harder and harder every year.

It was not so much the quality of the writing that struck me as particularly impressive; it was the fact that he asked to read the story aloud to me. I took that as a sign of great pride. Usually the students I shadowed offered to show me their work but never to read it aloud. In addition, Kevin refers specifically to the passion with which he wrote the portrait. Unlike the other work he did that received high marks, on this project he felt he truly deserved the A because he wrote from his heart. Though the grade was still a major focus, the writing was "real" for him and legitimate; he didn't cheat or kiss up or compromise, and so he felt his success was sweeter and more genuine.

Kevin discusses his community service project, PenPals, with the same kind of passion. He and a friend created the project freshman year as part of an assignment in their English class. The students were required to do ten hours of service, but Kevin and Ian spent more than 100 hours organizing students at the high school and a few local elementary schools to donate school supplies and clothing for children in the community who could not afford these necessities. This year they decided to continue and expand the project on their own—not for any course credit and not for a grade. Kevin notes with pride that he and his friends do the project without any adult sponsors or supervisors; "It's really kids helping kids directly . . . we do everything ourselves." And aside from some friendly advice from Ian's mother, this is true: The boys organized volunteer recruitment meetings and appointed site leaders. They contacted principals and parent teacher associations for approval. They supervised the distribution of collection bags to thirteen schools in the district, made promotional signs, and passed out 6,500 flyers. They appealed to local businesses and service organizations for help and received several thousand dollars' worth of supplies and in-kind donations. They collected all the bags (which literally filled a large meeting room at a nearby church) and spent the entire month of July sorting through the donated items. They collected so much, in fact, that they were featured in the city newspapers and broadcast news reports. Finally, at the end of the summer, they distributed the clothing and supplies to the schools that indicated they had students in need. In all, Kevin probably spent more than 200 hours working on PenPals, and plans to do it all again next year. He and Ian are even writing a handbook so the project can be a "legacy" to the school, and students can continue to run it after the boys graduate.

He explains the motivation behind the project:

> Community service is a big part of my life. I like it. It's fun. [I do it] to feel good about myself. Just to know I'm doing something to impact the community. . . . There's, like, studies that show that lack of school supplies, school necessities and proper clothing, contribute to the lack of self-esteem, which in turn contributes to the big thing about grades. . . . So if you get the problem early and help them with their self-esteem and help them get these common necessities that aren't that expensive, that aren't that hard to get, then you can in turn change them slightly.

In a later interview he adds that the rewards of helping others outweigh the typical rewards he receives in school:

KEVIN
ROMONI

I mean we are bringing joy to people and to ourselves, so that's why we do it, you know? No, we're not working for the recognition. We work for the fact that we like to help people, and it's a lot of work, like a job really, but we don't get paid, but it's worth it. . . .

I think I'm learning a lot more through PenPals than I actually would through high school. I mean, Pals, I mean it's like a business right now. I mean it's like we have to call people, we have to make contacts, we have to network, we have to, like, manage people, manage time, . . . and it's so much more than, the rewards are so much greater than grades. . . . You actually get to see, I mean a grade is a letter, but these people you're actually helping, do you know what I'm saying?

He points up to the newspaper articles written about the project that he has taped to the ceiling over his bed and says, "See I put that on my ceiling 'cause every morning I look up and I can feel good about myself."

Kevin does not post his transcript or his grade point average above his bed. These indicators of achievement do not mean as much to him and do not seem to make him feel as good about himself; rather, he values the work he does for the community above his school work for a number of reasons. He enjoys the opportunity to actually help, to make a difference in his community, to do something that feels real. He likes the fact that he can practice skills needed for business such as organizing people and managing his time. He likes that he and his friends can work together on the project without the help of adults. Kevin works as hard for PenPals and worries as much about the project as he does for his regular school work, except in this case, his motivation to do more than the minimum requirements appears to be intrinsic—it comes from the heart— and his work is rewarded in ways that are meaningful to him.

In fact, when imagining an ideal school, Kevin admits that he would like to see more projects done like PenPals that "matter" and that teach "people skills." He believes the real purpose of high school is to teach "life lessons like how to get along with others," lessons that he feels he has learned well so far and that will help him later in life. This is why he emphasizes in an earlier interview that he thinks he is a "good person, not a good student." He gets more pleasure out of helping people than out of achieving high grades.

KEVIN
ROMONI

When reflecting on the past semester and all the pressure to succeed, Kevin leaves the fantasy world of his ideal school and reverts back to his focus on grades. Success as a good person, it seems, is still not enough for Kevin to feel fulfilled. This time he compares himself to his friend Ian who struggles to maintain a 4.0 average and to balance several extracurricular activities on top of his academic load:

I balance a lot, but I just don't have as much as Ian. . . . I mean, I don't see how he does it, but he does, and more power to him. . . . But I wouldn't want that. I wouldn't want the kind of life Ian has. I've told him that before. Because I know that he's probably going to have more opportunities because of what he's doing right now, but he's not having any fun. . . . Because he's really scared to have fun because his whole life is just balancing on one little teeter totter thing, and like one little thing could throw it all off balance. My life's a lot better. I'd rather be me. I mean Ian's really smarter, he's in more honors classes, but—I don't care. I'd rather have fun and live life now, you know, and really have fun and do well at the same time. I like how I am now. I don't think I want to be classified as a 4.0 student; I would rather just be a 3.8 kind of guy.

When taken literally, it seems Kevin wants to be defined by his grade point average (one that is actually a bit higher than his current average). He admits that he feels pressure and must strive to balance his desires. He finds solace in the fact that at least he has more fun than his friend. He convinces himself that he can really "live life" (go to parties, goof off in class, hang out with his friends) and that this is a fair trade-off to getting a 4.0. Perhaps Kevin uses this as another excuse for why he is not fulfilling his potential (he'd rather live life than do the best he can in school), or as a way of competing with Ian (at least he has fun and does well enough). In any case, Kevin's actions belie the belief that he is happy to be a 3.8 kind of guy, and this attitude represents another strategy he uses to cope with the pressure.

His process for "doing school," thus, necessitates compromises. He feels obliged to choose conformity over authenticity in both his written assignments as well as his classroom behavior. He is compelled to emphasize external, future-oriented goals over personal satisfaction, except in the rare cases of doing community service and being able to attend parties while maintaining his high GPA, and— he attempts to convince himself that his behavior, if not genuine, is at least fairly "normal" and representative of the other students. "Everybody" does the minimum required to get by and everybody focuses on grades instead of learning the material. The pressure Kevin feels to succeed is his prime motivation, and though he doesn't like it, and it causes him occasional "breakdowns," he is resolved to rely on the strategies that have worked for him thus far. Until he hears messages from his parents, the school, and elsewhere that reward other kinds of behavior, Kevin will continue to work for the A's, if not for a 4.0, then for a 3.8. If he is unfulfilled, at least he can try to convince himself that he is having more fun than some of the other students he knows, students like Eve Lin in the following chapter.

CHAPTER 3

Eve Lin:
Life as a High School Machine

I was really stressed this weekend. I have a calculus test coming up, which means I have to do the homework for the past two weeks. I also have a physics quiz, which, of course, I was behind in that class by two chapters. So I played field hockey on Saturday with the team, and then did all the physics homework on Saturday and Sunday. Then I had two papers for English class. They are short papers, but still, I had to read the stories and then try to say something intellectual about them and relate them to my life. So I took No-Doze on Sunday night and kept drinking coffee, but I fell asleep writing my physics lab. A few hours later, at like 4 AM I woke up with a stomachache, but I had to do these papers, so I drank more coffee, and just kept writing. I had severe pains this morning which is probably like appendicitis or something, but look at me, I am still drinking coffee! I will finish the papers during lunch and then try to do all this stuff for ASB.[1] [She groans.] I swear I am not going to make it; I am going to die!

Junior year is "hell-year" for Eve Lin. Almost every week is "the worst" in her life, as she allows the endless demands of chapter tests, research projects, reading assignments, and study sessions to drive her to race through each day in a constant state of stress. She describes her life as one of "push, push, push," of "just surviving until June," and of literally working almost every moment of every day. She frequently does school work during brunch and lunch periods, and each night after dinner until the early morning hours. She "lives for" the weekends when she can catch up on all the homework that she could not complete during the week, and she spends her vacations working six or seven hours a day on school assignments. She admits that she is exhausted all the time, but that she can't help it: "This is just my work style. . . . This is how I do school."

Eve is overextended. She is enrolled in every available advanced placement and honors level course. She is a member of 12 school clubs and committees, including the School Site Council, the Associated Student Body, the Spanish Club, Junior Statesmen of America, the National Honors Society, and Mock Trial. She plays on the field hockey and badminton teams, and performs in two school bands. She boasts that she is ranked sixth in her class according to her grade point average and that she plans to keep this high ranking in order to get accepted to a top university. "The main purpose of high school," she explains, "is to prepare students for college" and, for Eve and her friends in particular, "to prepare for acceptance to the Ivy League."

She often dreams of a different kind of school life, one where she gets to "go home in the afternoon after playing a sport, and eat dinner, maybe watch an hour or two of TV, rest a bit, maybe have time to hang out with friends, and then do homework which you can finish in two hours." She "envies" students who have this life, "students who are in college prep classes and who will probably go to fairly good schools."[2] But she is sure that these students will never get into Ivy League colleges, and this is not an acceptable option for her. Eve wants to go "as high as [she] can go." She wants to go to Harvard.

EVE
LIN

Eve acquired this philosophy at an early age. She completed four years of school in Taiwan, and she remembers the atmosphere there as very strict, competitive, and "completely focused on academics." When she came to the United States, she worked hard in her English as a Second Language (ESL) classes and learned English well enough to be mainstreamed into regular classes by fifth grade. By the time she finished middle school, she had won the 25 dollar reward for achieving a perfect grade point average two years in a row. (She explains that the reward would have been higher, except she had to share the money with the ten other 4.0 students in her class that year, "many of whom were also Asian.")[3]

When she began high school, Eve constantly worried about grades and college acceptances. She had planned to maintain her perfect grade point average throughout the four years, but during one of her final exams freshman year, something "terrible" happened:

> I needed to get a 98 on my math final to get an A in the class. But, as it turns out, I only got a 95 which gave me a B+ for the year. At first I was devastated, like, "How could this happen to me?" But sometimes I think it is good because I don't have to worry about maintaining a 4.0. I mean some of my friends are really freaking out about this, and I can just laugh at them because I don't need to worry.

Eve repeats this story several times during the semester. She tries to convince me (and apparently herself) that she is not overly con-

EVE
LIN

cerned about her grades because she has already "ruined" her average by getting a B. However, rather than freeing Eve of such worries, the "low" grade on her math exam actually seems to have increased her anxiety. She sees it as a blight on her record that makes her appear, "lesser in [her] friends' eyes—like not an equal anymore." She finds some solace when she hears from friends that "freshman grades don't really count [on college transcripts]," and resolves to work harder to keep up with her high-achieving peers. Her current 3.97 GPA, along with her high class ranking, attests to her success.

Over and over again I ask Eve, "Why are you doing this? Why push so hard?" And each time she replies with the same answer:

> To get into an Ivy. That's all I can think about . . . to get in and become a successful $500,000-a-year doctor or engineer or whatever it is I want to be. . . . It's very narrow-minded for me. . . . I have to get accepted; then I can have a life, once I'm in. . . .

Of this goal, Eve seems sure. However, she is less clear when she ponders the reasons behind the goal. She says on one occasion that it is her choice to take on such a difficult course load. Another time she says she feels forced to conform—that her parents, her friends, her "environment," the school—all are pushing her toward the "Ivy League route." At the end of the year, she wavers again: "I choose to go for the maximum. . . . I do it to myself. I don't want to be this busy, but then I don't think I would be happy if I was a major slacker. I worked my way up, and I am proud of the results."

It is true that her hard work has earned her high marks and the respect of teachers, peers, and administrators. The principal calls Eve a "real star," and one teacher tells me that Eve is an "ideal student;" in fact, he wishes "more students had her academic dedication." However, Eve's demanding work style and "narrow-mindedness" takes a severe toll on her health and social life. She fails to recognize the large gap that exists between "working every minute" and being a "major slacker." Indeed, Eve's "academic dedication" results in some consequences that hardly seem "ideal."

"Going for the Maximum"

Unlike Kevin's success strategy of "doing the minimum to get by," Eve chooses to "go for the maximum," often doing extra work for a few more points on her transcript. While her peers bring in half a page of sketchy notes or no notes at all to a discussion on Martin Luther King Jr.'s "Letter from Birmingham Jail," Eve shows me two typed pages on the use of themes and stylistic devices in the piece that she's written for extra credit. She also opts to re-write her English papers to change the A− grades to A's, and, by doing so, is praised by her teacher for showing such a "commitment to excellence." In her Spanish presentations, she almost always employs elaborate visual aids and runs over the thirty minute time limit, while her classmates struggle to find even fifteen minutes' worth of material to discuss. Furthermore, in her AP history class, when she knows that she has a 99 at the end of the year, and that she could get a D+ on the final and still have an A grade on her transcript, Eve chooses to spend her whole weekend studying for the exam. She explains her strategy:

> This is the way I have always done my work. I think if I spend any time on it, I might as well turn in like the best I can, and also it gives the teacher an impression of you. . . . For me it's always been, like, it's not that much more difficult to do a better job. It takes about one or two extra hours or whatever, and then the

EVE
LIN
teacher also respects you more and sees that you're not a slacker. Then it's also the relationship with the teacher is better too, because the teacher thinks that you're taking his or her class seriously.

One or two extra hours to another student may seem like an eternity, but to Eve, it is time well spent for the difference between an A− and an A, or maybe even an A+. Besides, if she pleases the teacher, he may write her a better college recommendation.

Such a strategy, however, comes with severe consequences. Because Eve is enrolled in so many advanced courses and serves on so many committees and clubs, she cannot possibly do everything she needs to do and still, as she puts it, "have a life." Instead of seeking some sort of balance between work and play, as Kevin believes he does, Eve chooses to focus solely on her school commitments at the expense of an active social life, and often at the expense of her health as well. She explains:

> I sometimes have two or three days where I only get two hours of sleep per night. I see lots of my friends burned out, but I don't have time to worry about this. . . . It's the typical Asian way. Lots of us are getting sick, and I am addicted to coffee; actually, I prefer to say voluntarily dependent on caffeine. See, some people see health and happiness as more important than grades and college; I don't. I feel compelled to compete because we have a really smart class, and I am competing with them to get into college.

Eve is not exaggerating here. On several occasions she and her friends drag themselves through the school day, puffy-eyed and haggard, only to face another evening of more homework and very little sleep. At the end of the year when most of the big projects and reports were due, Eve, along with many of the top students in the class, became quite ill. She complained of frequent stomach-aches, heartburn, and an "acid-taste" on her tongue. She said she wasn't eating well—just "surviving on cereal" because she literally didn't have time for meals, and she was usually "too stressed and tired to feel hungry."

EVE
LIN

Eve's health became so poor at times that her parents started to worry about her. She told me that her father believed she had an ulcer and that he asked her to "cut back" on some of her activities so she could have more time to sleep. Twice during the semester, when Eve fell asleep while working at her desk at home, her mother decided not to wake her up to go to school that day. Instead, she met with Eve's teachers to excuse these absences and to pick up any work she may have missed. Eve appreciated the kind gesture from her mother but felt trapped by her parents' demands to slow down: "They are worried about me and say that it's okay if I don't go to an Ivy school, like they'll still be proud of me, but that's b.s. because no they won't." In the same conversation Eve says:

> If I quit something, I will consider myself a failure, and I really really fear failure. Afterwards I think, "Oh that wasn't that bad." It was okay; I mean I am not dead yet. . . . I mean certainly I never got to the extent of some of my friends who get so stressed and tired that they talk about suicide. I mean I was never like *that*, you know. . . . In fact most of the time I am really proud that I was able to withstand all the stress. It makes me a stronger person, and, like, next time I know I will be able to deal with it and not break down. I think high school really builds up your tolerance for stress.[4]

Eve believes that withstanding this stress will make her "a stronger person," yet physically (and mentally at times), she seems on the verge of collapsing. Surely, such consequences are not intentional on the part of the school or her parents, yet Eve receives mixed messages from both sources. On the one hand, the school purposely schedules certain courses at the same time, so, according to Eve, students cannot enroll in all of them and "get too stressed out." Students, for instance, must choose between writing for the school newspaper, publishing the yearbook, and serving on the Associated Student Body. They are also allowed to take only one advanced placement level science class at a time, and they must pass rigorous prerequisite qualifications for honors classes—to ensure, as one teacher explains, "that no one gets in over [his or her] head."[5] The students, however, seem to have enough to worry about in spite of these precautions. The course limits in science are the exception to the rule, as the school course guide suggests "typical pathways for exceptional students" that include honors level and advanced placement courses in almost every subject area. Moreover, students like Eve are prominently featured on the student honors board located outside the school office, and many receive monthly departmental awards for their academic success that serve to reinforce the importance of achieving high grades.

Eve's parents join her teachers in praising her outstanding school work. Eve hears them brag to their friends and relatives in Taiwan about her many awards and her high grade point average. So, naturally, when her parents tell her to "cut back," Eve doubts their real intent. She has heard messages of "future success" from too many sources for too long. She has become used to the accolades and the limelight and has grown to fear failure, so much so that she is willing to exchange "health and happiness" for acceptance to an Ivy League college. Her diligence and commitment may appear to be that of the ideal student, especially compared to those students who rarely do homework or show little concern for their future, but beneath the high GPA and the "packed" résumé, lies a tired and worried teenager with "no life." Eve says, "I am just a machine with no life at this place. . . . This school turns students into robots. I have been thinking about it a lot; I am a robot just going page by page, doing the work, doing the routine."

School, for Eve, is lifeless; her grueling routine leaves little time for anything else. For example, one day during Spirit Week on campus, the school secretary gave Eve a water balloon. Eve was very busy and couldn't decide what to do with the balloon, so she handed it to a friend. Five minutes later, neither girl could decide what to do with the balloon, and, as they discussed the calculus problem set, Eve eventually threw the balloon away in a nearby trash can. She was so focused on her math problems that she could not be bothered by such frivolity. Later she told me, "I want to have fun, just not at the expense of school."

Survival of the Fittest

In her tenth grade biology class, when Eve learned about Darwin's theory of evolution and the concept of "survival of the fittest," she immediately related the theory to her own life. She explains, "I love that theory because that's the way my group of friends are." The ones who manage to "stay up and take as much stress as possible and still stay alive" are the most fit and "stay on top and survive." But the ones who can't "take all the pressure and the intensity. . . . They are not on top anymore." The whole point is to "beat each other and rise above."

Eve admits that such a theory seems "harsh" and "cruel," but she believes that one must have this mindset in order to get into the best universities:

EVE
LIN

A person who wants to go to Ivy League knows the ideal goals, . . . and you get so caught up in like this conflict preparing for it . . . that you realize, "Oh wait I'm competing with all these other students too." And the college can only accept a certain amount of people from a school, you know, and . . . so you start competing with them, kind of hiding things from them.

Eve understands the intense competition to get accepted to an Ivy League school. She also realizes that she and her friends are very much alike. Most are high-achieving, intelligent, and talented Chinese students who often participate in the same school clubs and enroll in the same advanced courses. She believes that she must set herself apart from her friends in some way to "catch the attention" of the admissions committees and rise above her peers, so she engages in secretive behavior to hide those activities she believes will distinguish her. For example, she hides the fact that she volunteers at a local hospital each week, hoping that this community service will somehow set her apart. She also tries not to reveal much information about a special math class at a local college that she plans to take in the summer, praying that her friends won't find out about it in time to register. Finally, she and her friends are secretive about their grades, pretending they didn't do as well as they had hoped on a paper or exam, thereby attempting to divert attention away from themselves and onto another top student. Usually, though, the students discover the truth by sneaking glances at the graded paper or counting down the alphabetical rows of posted grades on the classroom wall to discover their friends' scores.

Despite the intense competition among her friends, Eve says they are also her main source of support. They go to each other's games and recitals, they buy flowers and candy to cheer each other up, and they listen to one another complain about the workload

and the exhaustion they face. Eve notes the irony within their relationships:

> In one sense, we are very competitive and we don't want the
> other one to beat us . . . but we also really understand what we
> are all going through and the pressure we are undergoing, . . . so
> we push each other because we know we are all capable of going
> to the best colleges, and we just kind of like cheer for the other
> one. . . . Sometimes it is cut-throat and we don't tell each other
> what we are doing, and we are always looking for ways to prove
> we are better than them . . . but then we will email each other late
> at night and say, "How's it going?"

As the school system has been constructed, this kind of love-hate
relationship between peers seems necessary to achieve the results
Eve desires; when students from the same school compete for a few
spaces in a particular university, when students are graded on a
curve where only some can achieve an A, when classrooms are set
up to reinforce competition between students (by posting the A papers on the board or announcing the top test scorers, or by allowing the top five percent of the class to skip the final exam), students
are often forced to choose between cheering on their friends or
plotting against them.[6] Even in the classrooms that emphasize cooperative learning and group work (which many of the advanced
courses do), Eve feels her loyalty torn. She knows that ultimately
the teacher must assign individual grades, and she wants hers to be
the best.

Eve mentions the same conflicting emotions when she describes
the practice of cheating among her friends. Clearly, with the intense
competition and stress the students face, the temptation to cheat is
strong, and Eve admits that many of her friends engage in some
cheating behavior. She is upset by this deceptive conduct because

EVE
LIN

"they get A's without studying as much," while she "works her butt off for the same grade." But she does not report this behavior to the authorities. She does not want to get her friends in trouble or hurt their chances for college acceptance, even though she believes some of the things they do are "completely immoral."

I notice, in fact, that most of the advanced students do not cheat in the ways the students in other tracks do. I see very little copying of others' answers during tests or use of cheat sheets. Instead, as Eve points out (and I observe), the advanced students cheat by programming equations into their calculators, cutting classes on the day of the exam to gain more studying time, and asking friends who took the exam earlier that day about specific material and questions. This behavior, according to Eve, "screws over the honest students because the teacher never changes the test and grades everyone on the same curve." Eve prides herself on never using any of these tactics to get ahead. She is determined to "work [her] way to the top the right way, the honest way, by not cheating or cutting class," even if this means she may not be the school valedictorian. And in the eight months that I observe her, this is true; she does not "cheat" according to her definition of the word.

What I do observe, however, is the use of various strategies that some educators may qualify as cheating but that the students believe are perfectly acceptable. I often notice Eve and her friends sharing homework answers and checking problem sets together. Eve also regularly copies the answers to calculus problems from the board and then turns them in as her own work. She whispers answers to friends during class question-and-answer sessions and gratefully accepts help from her neighbors when she is called on during discussions. Eve does not construe this behavior as cheating; instead she insists that "comparing and discussing answers for homework or during class discussions is okay. The teachers want us to work together." One teacher tells me later that this is a "tough call." He encourages students to share strategies on problem sets, but he ultimately wants the work they turn in to be their own. Eve and her friends have decided that the line here is unclear. Because they cannot possibly do all the assignments by themselves, they have created a "cooperative" learning environment to help them get through the mounds of work. Here, as is typical with these students, the focus is on getting good grades, rather than on actually learning the material.

EVE
LIN

In addition to these creative but somewhat deceitful strategies, Eve relies on other tactics to help her achieve success. In many of her classes, she consciously strives to appear as if she is paying attention, even though in reality she may be doing other homework assignments or studying for exams. For instance, she tries to ask a question "every ten minutes or so" in her science class so the teacher will think she is on task. In between these moments of attention she manages to write two journal entries for English class. When the science teacher calls on her without warning a few minutes later, Eve is able to answer his question correctly. I see her do this on several occasions, even in her difficult classes such as calculus. When asked about this impressive feat, she replies:

> I have a talent for listening out of both of my ears. I can carry on a conversation with a friend or work on homework and still know what's going on at the board. . . . I can also tell when they're going to ask a question and I start to pay attention.

She has learned the right time to "tune-out" and on which days she should "sit in the front of the class and really concentrate." In this sense, Eve has become the "consummate" student. She has learned to use almost every moment in school to her advantage, at times even photocopying pages of her history text so she can study without the danger of being caught in calculus with the wrong book on her desk.

Eve engages in other subterfuge as well. Though she believes ditching class to study for a test is "immoral," she has no problem cutting classes for other reasons such as going home to print out her Spanish paper or taking a long lunch with friends after a particularly exhausting morning of exams. She simply makes up an excuse ("I have a counseling appointment") or informs the teacher that she will miss class "for a really important reason" but promises to make up any missed work. The teachers trust Eve because she does well in their classes, because she is a student leader in the school, and because she works hard to maintain a friendly relationship with them. She laughs as she zooms out of the parking lot during fourth period, "They would never think I would be doing anything like cutting a class!"

Like Kevin, Eve consciously attempts to win favor with her teachers and the school administrators. She tries to "dress nicely" when she comes to school to "make a good impression." "After all," she exclaims, "you never know when you will have an important meeting or interview where you need to look mature." She also chooses to be on "highly visible" committees so the principal and vice principals will get to know her. The strategies obviously pay off as Eve brags:

> I am so in with the administration, I can get away with so much it's pathetic. Even my friends sometimes ask me to approach administrators for favors for them. Like last week I missed the deadline for the AP checks, so I got the bookkeeper to give me an extension. See, it helps to know people and for them to know me.

One day she cut class to buy the two school secretaries some giant yellow sunflowers. She told me that she feels very close to them because they help her all the time. They allow her to use their phones

and computers and to study at their desks when they are not
busy. Once, when Eve was very stressed about missing a deadline
for a scholarship application, one of the secretaries offered to
type the essay for her. In turn, Eve obliges a favor when she can; for
example, she agreed to help a new Taiwanese student's family communicate with the district office.

Eve's visibility at the school gains her other advantages as well.
Because she has served on several committees with school personnel, she feels comfortable stating her mind and challenging various
school decisions. She regularly contests grades that she believes are
unfair (though often this contesting wins her only a point or two),
and twice she has appealed teachers' decisions that could have prevented her from taking honors level courses. Both times, she went
above the teachers' heads and convinced an administrator to allow
her to re-take the entrance exams, which she then passed, and was
admitted into the courses. She even engaged in a one-on-one fight
with the Academic Vice Principal for the right to enroll in multiple
advanced placement science courses. As noted above, the school
usually forbids this practice, but after several meetings Eve prevailed
and was allowed to enroll, giving her a grand (and unprecedented)
total of seven advanced placement courses during her senior year.

Happy with the results of her battle, Eve nonetheless felt frustrated that her friends did not join her in the fight, especially since
they too would have been allowed to take the multiple advanced
courses, thanks to her efforts. She pleaded with them to attend
meetings with her or write letters of support, but they claimed to
be too busy or they feared repercussions with the administration.
Eve pressed harder, telling them that "at some point in their lives
they will be working with people who are older and smarter, and
they will need to take a stand and fight for what they want." But her
friends did not share Eve's passion; nor did they share her close ties

with the school personnel. In this sense, Eve has distinguished herself from her peers. She has achieved a position of power in the school, one which allows her to voice opinions and be heard. Although she regrets that she cannot "command as much respect as some parents or teachers," she vows to keep on fighting for her needs at the school. "It's *my* education," she says, "They [administrators] usually get the final say, but I am here to remind them that they are supposed to be watching out for *me*."

Such conviction and passion is rare in my observations of the advanced students. Most tend to placate teachers and administrators since the adults wield power in the form of grades and college recommendations. Eve may not be as sugary sweet and polite as Kevin, for instance, but she achieves similar results. The teachers know her, respect her, and accord her the advantages that go along with winning their trust. Thus, in the survival game, Eve seems to have adapted well to her environment and has secured a place among the most "fit."

Enjoying the Process

At the end of the school year, Eve receives a letter from a friend at MIT. He wrote that he realized "too late into his senior year of high school" that he "regretted the focus on competing for an Ivy League school." He advised Eve: "If you are going to go for the result, you might as well enjoy the process of getting there, and then if you don't get the result you actually want, at least be satisfied that you enjoyed yourself."

I ask Eve if she can honestly say she "enjoyed the process" this year. She replies that she "loved" doing some of her extracurricular activities such as "Mock Trial and coordinating the activity cards[7] for ASB." She explains that she was surprised by how much she enjoyed these activities, especially since they were both "so stressful."

At first I did [Mock Trial] mostly because my mom told me it would look good on my transcript, but then it was just really exciting. You know you go up there and you are with a real judge . . . in a real courtroom . . . and you go up there and you present this case. Like you hear about the O. J. Simpson case and think . . . oh, I don't understand it, but then when you actually start preparing for this kind of process, you actually understand bits and pieces of . . . the court system and what's going on in the community. **EVE LIN**

Eve appreciated the "real life" aspect of her activity card work as well. She says the ASB project represented one of her "biggest risks this year," because the school usually contracts with an outside company to create and sell the activity cards. Eve figured that the school would make more money by creating the cards "in-house" and selling advertisement and coupon space on the back of the cards to local food and retail stores. The money from the sales would help defray costs of school activities, and local stores would benefit from an increase in student patronage. She had several meetings with the principal where she "sold him" on the idea and then met with the district's Assistant Superintendent to work out the details. She boasted that she got to meet with the Assistant Superintendent "all by [herself]" and that she only needed to change "one clause" in the contract she had written for the potential vendors. The best aspect for Eve was that she "had the power to . . . make a change . . . and to interact with big people on campus." Like Kevin, Eve enjoyed engaging with an activity that could make a difference in the community. She felt empowered by the opportunity to play a role normally reserved for an adult and enjoyed the fact that she could take a "real" risk (in terms of the school's money as well as her own reputation) and emerge successful.

The other time Eve spoke with such pride in her accomplishments was after her presentation on the history of NASA Apollo missions. The students worked with their friends in groups of three or four to do intensive research on a topic in American history. They were supposed to present their findings in a "well-organized, highly creative, multi-media, educational and entertaining" hour-long presentation that comprised the joint English and history classes' semester project. Eve's group met and did research together for more than 250 hours before their final presentation. Each group tried to out-perform the ones who went before them, and Eve's group, the last one of the day, delivered, by far, the best presentation I had seen. The following excerpt from field notes conveys the magnitude of the students' presentation:

> Teachers, students, and the District Superintendent, who are here to see the group presentations, enter the darkened room to the booming sound of Star Wars music. The walls are covered from floor to ceiling with dark sheets and silver twinkling stars. All four group members wear NASA name tags and t-shirts, and we are handed a NASA spacecraft center visitor pass as we walk through the door. At the front of the room are three large computer terminals, a large-screen television set, and four sets of six-foot speakers, creating a surround-sound effect. . . . During the hour the students make several scene and costume changes as they take the audience on a fact-filled journey of the various Apollo rockets. We are on the launchpad; we are at the NASA museum; we are "with" the astronauts via a video montage of real NASA footage, Hollywood clips of space travel, and a student-made video of what life is like in space. . . . The music blasts and the computers beep madly as the rockets take off. Now the audience is assigned the task of constructing plug filters needed to

take the Apollo 13 crew safely home. We tape together card-
board cones and rubber hoses and styrofoam cups to simu-
late what the astronauts needed to do. . . . At the end of the
hour the audience "grades" the presentation. Several students
whisper that it deserves an A. The teacher gives the group an A+,
calling the presentation "magnificent."

EVE

LIN

Afterward, the group is pleased with the teacher's grade, but they
are more excited that the student whom they describe as the
"toughest critic in the class" has awarded them an A. They take this
to be "an extreme compliment," because he usually gives no higher
than a B grade. Perhaps Eve and her friends have become so used
to receiving high grades from their teachers, that good marks from
them have become routine. But when a proven "tough critic" com-
mends their work, it truly means something.

While she cleans the room and takes down the set, Eve tells me
that despite the good grade, she is a little disappointed with the results of the project:

> To be honest, it went as well as I hoped; I mean we got the A, but
> it's a little anticlimactic. I guess with all the work I hoped maybe
> we could do it for other periods or teach younger kids at an ele-
> mentary school assembly about NASA. All that work for a one-
> hour performance. . . . I mean I am glad because I learned a lot,
> and I am really proud of all of us, but it is a little sad. Like the Su-
> perintendent was so impressed with our use of technology and
> stuff. I think people really underestimate what students can do.
> We could do more with this presentation.

Eve's pride in the performance is tempered by her regret that she
couldn't "do more" with the presentation, and she feels unfulfilled.

EVE
LIN

It is one of the few times that she realizes she wants more from her high school education than simply "getting the grades."

Such sentiment is short-lived, however. One day after the performance, Eve hears that some students are upset about her group's use of genuine NASA material. They complain that it is unfair that Eve's group had access to NASA and received video clips and uniforms normally off-limits to the general public. Eve shrugs and replies: "Yeah, we had connections. That's life—it's all about connections—who you know. Kind of like how I know all the secretaries in the office. What can I say? That's how you get what you need." Hence, even while Eve searches for greater fulfillment (beyond grades and college acceptances), she remains constantly aware of playing the game and getting what she needs. Though she thoroughly enjoys some of her school activities, she knows their ultimate value: her Mock Trial work looks great on her transcript; her activity card innovation pleased the school administrators and gave her an "in" with the district office; and her NASA project won her an A grade, in part, due to a connection through her friend's father who worked there.

Eve struggles to find an activity she does "just for [herself]." She tells me that she reads Chinese philosophy in both English and Chinese "just for fun." Although she was introduced to some of the texts in Chinese school, an extracurricular private school which she attends once a week to learn Chinese language, culture, and cuisine, she says she has "moved ahead of the class" and tries to "squeeze in fifteen minutes here and there" to read her favorite philosophers.[8] She enjoys the reading because she can learn more about her "cultural heritage," and she already has books on Confucius, Laoism, and Taoism on her summer reading list.

This summer Eve plans to teach science to middle school students, write her college essays, apply for several scholarships, read

her required literature for AP English, attend the Girls' State
convention, and, she whispers, "take that special math class" at
the community college ("don't tell anyone!"). She shakes her
head when she realizes how busy she will be: "I don't know why I
do this to myself." She pauses for a moment then adds—contra-
dicting an earlier statement, "I don't think I would enjoy going
home, watching TV, doing an hour of homework. . . . I need to be
active, to feel like I really accomplished something. . . . Call me
crazy, but I actually love being pushed."

Like Kevin who tries to convince himself that he is somehow
"having fun" in his pursuit for a high GPA, sacrificing a possible 4.0
to "go to parties and live life," Eve tries to convince herself that she
wouldn't be happy doing school any other way. Ultimately, however, Eve cannot hide her frustration and disappointment with
some of her achievements. She resents her life as a school robot and
the tactics she must use to get ahead. She wants to believe that she
has chosen this route to success freely, but she recognizes the outside pressures that have influenced her. She hopes that ultimately
college acceptance and the future benefits that accompany admission to an Ivy League institution will prove that her efforts have
been worthwhile; until then, she knows she will have to give up
sleep, good health, and a social life in order to maintain her ranking as one of the top students in the class.

CHAPTER 4

Teresa Gomez:
"I Want a Future"

Teresa Gomez races into her first period Spanish class and checks the clock on the wall: 8:25 AM; she is 25 minutes late and has missed half of the period. "Lo siento, Señora," she blurts out in Spanish as she tries to catch her breath, "I am so sorry, but I had to take my cousin to the hospital, and I was the only one at home who could drive, and she was very, very sick." The teacher glances at Teresa for a brief moment, waves her hand toward the door, and continues with the lesson. Teresa understands the gesture and walks across campus to the office to get a tardy slip. She appears to know the routine well since it is her seventh time being tardy this month. Upon returning to class, she digs through her backpack for her Spanish book and frowns when she realizes she has left it at home with the worksheet due that day. Her eyes well-up with tears and she tells me she has a headache. With a whisper, she borrows a pen-cil from the student sitting next to her and tries to focus on the teacher's lecture. Minutes later she sneezes loudly, jumps to her feet, and grabs some Kleenex from the box on the teacher's desk. Embarrassed by her sneeze, she stands in the doorway, her back to the class, attempting quietly to blow her nose without attracting any more attention. Once seated, she twists her long, brown hair into a bun, lowers her head in her hands and moans softly, "Oooh. I don't feel good. I should go home."

TERESA
GOMEZ

Teresa seems to spend almost half of the semester blowing her nose in classroom doorways. Her health problems lead to a number of absences and cause her to experience school through a perpetual flu-induced fog. She "can't understand why [she is] sick so much," but she is "too busy to see a doctor." She explains that she doesn't sleep many hours or eat well because she has a "very crazy schedule," and "lots of things interfere with school." Homework competes with her paying job and family obligations. During a typical lunch of Doritos and Diet Pepsi, Teresa explains that it is "difficult to be the only child in a Mexican family. I don't have no sisters or no brothers, so I am expected to help. They need me to help."

She lives with her mother and her mother's boyfriend in a small downtown apartment that often houses several relatives making the transition from Mexico to the United States. This semester, Teresa shares her room with her aunt and her five-month-old nephew. She shakes her head and says with a sigh, "Nobody sleeps when the baby cries." Because her mother works every day, Teresa is called on to drive relatives to job interviews and doctor appointments, and these responsibilities often cause her to be late to her first period classes. She misses one full day of school a month in order to accompany her mother to "medical treatments" at a clinic two hours away, and because her mother and other relatives don't speak English very well, Teresa serves as a translator during meet-

TERESA
GOMEZ

ings with landlords, insurance agents, and lawyers. These family commitments seem to take place at the worst possible times for Teresa; the night before a biology unit test, for example, she spent three hours arguing with her mother's landlord about a lost rent check.

Teresa's job at a local Mexican restaurant also impinges on her study time. She works as a cashier approximately 35 hours a week (Wednesday, Thursday, and Friday from 4 to 10 PM, and full-time on the weekends), which leaves only a few hours on Monday and Tuesday evenings to do most of her homework. Her mother wants her to quit or cut down to fewer hours because she sees the toll it takes on her daughter, but Teresa refuses; she is saving the money she earns to replace her broken and outdated IBM computer. She enjoys her job because she "likes the people" and because her boss occasionally allows her to work in the main office and "learn accounting," a field she eventually hopes to enter. As she describes the office work, her eyes light up:

> I do filing and database entry for them on Excel which I wish we were learning here [at school], but we don't. In the office I learn about payroll and paying vendors. My boss teaches me. He really expanded the business. He owns three chains by hisself. He's really smart because he makes a lot of money because the food is really expensive and they pay the employees not too much, so he makes lots of money because rice and beans and chicken cost, don't cost much from the vendors. . . . I also want to make lots of money like my boss one day, so that's why I want to be an accountant.

Like Kevin and Eve, Teresa is enticed by the possibility of making "lots of money" and sees her education as a means toward that end. She becomes so excited about a career in accounting that she enrolls in a new "business theme house" (Business House) where she takes English, history, and computer courses focused around business issues. The 28 students in this program take these three core courses together and participate in monthly field trips to various companies to learn basic business principles and to explore "potential career opportunities" (FHS Course Guide, p. 6). The students are also paired with adult mentors who offer support in learning business technology skills and give advice on interviewing and résumé writing.

TERESA GOMEZ

In addition to business courses, Teresa takes math, Spanish, biology, and Mexican dance. She does not need to take all seven courses this year,[1] especially with her busy home and work schedule, but Teresa chooses to take the elective class, dance, "for two reasons": she gets "PE credit" for the course, and she "enjoys learning about Mexican history and tradition—because it's important if you're Mexican to learn about your country." The class is taught mostly in Spanish, and all but one of the students come from Mexico or have Mexican parents. They eat lunch together in the cafeteria and spend most of their break periods together, always meeting at the same spot near the stage. Many are part of the Mexican student association where the dance teacher serves as advisor, and where they spend the majority of their time planning an elaborate school-wide Cinco de Mayo celebration. In April and May, Teresa spent more than 40 hours outside of school helping to plan the celebration, not counting the time she spent rehearsing dances to be performed at the school assembly that day. The students decorated the cafeteria with large murals depicting scenes from Mexico; they made beautiful tablecloths and costumes, prepared and served traditional tamales and rice, sold tickets to raise money for college scholarships for the dancers, and eventually

TERESA
GOMEZ

convinced more than 100 people to stand up and join them in their celebratory dances.

Membership in the dance class and student association is central to Teresa's school experience. She spends time thinking about her next performance (they perform about 15 times a year) and silently practicing dance moves while sitting at her desk in algebra or biology class, her feet moving left and right as she taps out a Mexican rhythm. She remembers the thrill of dancing in front of the whole school as a little girl in Mexico, and though she describes herself as "very shy," I have seen her calm her nerves and smile widely at the large audiences for whom she performs. She struggles to express in words how she feels when she dances, but her face and body language show a spark and enthusiasm that is rare in her other courses.

Dancing as Engagement

It is the last period of the day and Teresa is clearly exhausted. She rubs her red, puffy eyes and drags herself to the cafeteria where students in her dance class are practicing various moves on stage before the teacher arrives. Teresa yawns and steps into a multi-layered, brightly colored skirt, leaving the bottom of her flared jeans exposed beneath the skirt's lacy hemline. She tells me she is both "excited and stressed" about the upcoming Mexican dance conference in Southern California. She is worried about missing classes and finishing her history report, but she had "such a good time" at last year's conference that she can't wait for the weekend to arrive. She turns to blow her nose, tucks extra Kleenex in her waistband, and joins the others on the stage.

The teacher walks in and immediately calls the class to attention. She turns on the music and watches carefully as the students rehearse the six different dances for the conference without taking a single break. She does not tolerate any chatting or goofing around, not when they have only a few more practices left before the big day. She yells in Spanish that they must remember to smile, raise their heads, think about timing. When Teresa gets lost in the middle of "the bird dance," the teacher reprimands her: "Teresa, donde estás hoy? [Where are you today?]." She uses the Spanish pronunciation of Teresa's name, the one where the middle "e" sounds like the "a" in "way," the pronunciation used by Teresa's close friends and family. Teresa struggles with the moves but manages to laugh at the end when she winds up on the wrong side of her partner. She looks at her frowning teacher and borrows a copy of the music, promising to practice the dance at home this evening.

After the grueling workout, the students gulp water from the fountain as the teacher sets up the VCR. Two minutes later, the television screen shows professional dancers in elaborate costumes seamlessly performing the same dances the students rehearsed. "Mira! Watch," says the teacher, "I want you to look like this. Notice the arms." Teresa talks excitedly to her friend (in Spanish) about copying the professional dresses and jewelry for the competition and asks if the teacher will take them out to dinner after the conference "like last year." "Only if you do the dances *perfectly*," the teacher replies with a smile, and the students buzz with anticipation. The bell rings and Teresa says with surprise, "The bell already? Man, that was fast." She tells the teacher she can stay only an extra hour after school to practice because she must go to work. The teacher frowns at Teresa for the second time that day. The class usually runs from one to three hours, depending on when the next public performance is scheduled, and today she needs everyone to stay late. Despite the teacher's complaints,

Teresa and two other boys who have jobs leave class "early," an hour after the bell rings.

For Teresa, this dance class is "completely different" from her other courses at school. In this class she loses track of time, often rushing off to work after noticing the late hour; in other classes she cranes her head to watch the clock and complains about the slow pace. In this class she speaks quickly in her native tongue, giggling with her friends, while in other classes she is quiet, shy, and "embarrassed by [her] Mexican accent." Here, she works hard to learn the dance moves, not showing signs of frustration or panic or anger when she makes mistakes or is slow to catch on. She usually just shakes her head, watches her partner closely, and tries the steps again. And whereas she criticizes many of her other teachers, Teresa has only praise for her dance teacher: "She is tough and strict in a good way. She makes us work, like she pushes us, but after the performance she won't say anything negative, like she say, 'Oh you were great, you were wonderful,' even if we were so-so."

Teresa wishes she could feel as good about her other classes. She began the year with high expectations for improving her English and for learning business and technology skills in the Business House program. In fact, one of the school counselors recommended Teresa for this study precisely because she took "concrete steps" toward improving her school experience early in the year: Teresa was one of the first students to volunteer for the new business program, and she made a special request to transfer into a different math class after the first quarter when she realized the teacher "wasn't explaining things in a way she could understand." The counselor was impressed by Teresa's "commitment to her academic goals." As the semester progressed, Teresa made it clear to me and others that her expectations were not being fulfilled. She grew frustrated with her classes and complained that she "wanted more out of school."

"Wanting More": The Search for Engagement

TERESA
GOMEZ

THE DESIRE TO LEARN ENGLISH

One of the main sources of Teresa's frustration was her difficulty with the English language. Arriving from Mexico in the fourth grade, Teresa was placed in an English as a Second Language class for an hour and a half each day. The rest of her elementary school experience was spent in English-speaking classrooms with mostly native speakers. She remembers feeling "lost and confused" and "frustrated" that she could not "get the A's and B's [she] got in Mexico." She particularly remembers the "loneliness" of "feeling like a weirdo" because she did not know the language. She recalls one incident in particular that still haunts her:

> At the beginning when I start to learn English, I don't know but this happened in elementary. I was barely starting to learn and then this girl just laughed at a word that I said, and I think that affected like my thinking, a lot of years, it was, I was shy for many years. I learn English but never practice it . . . 'cause I think pupils all the times poke fun at me now, I think they might make fun of me. And I am with my friends speaking Spanish and my family, so I don't practice.

Teresa's situation is fairly common. She prefers the company of Spanish-speaking friends and uses her native language at home as well, leaving little time for practicing English (Davidson, 1996). Consequently, she worries about her accent and tries to avoid speaking English in public. For example, she was supposed to summarize a newspaper article on a "current business event" for her English class. After hearing a friend's presentation, Teresa pleaded with the teacher to give her more time to prepare: "I can't go yet! She made me too nervous. She was so good. Please pick someone else." The teacher refused, and after Teresa nervously stammered her way through the report, she sat down and said, "Oh, God, that was terrible." A friend tried to console her, "No way, that was an A plus, Teresa, A plus." Teresa looked at her and laughed, as if to say, "We both know that wasn't even close to an A." Later, she showed me a handout on communication skills from her computer teacher. Teresa had underlined the sentence: "How you say what you say accounts for 70 percent of how you are evaluated." She explained, "This is my goal for school; I don't know, I am not sure, um, if I want to go to a four-year [college], but I want to know more and be able to speak good and answer all questions like that [she gives a quick snap of her fingers]."

Though Teresa's language skills are not nearly as weak as she believes them to be,[2] they do noticeably slow her down at times, especially in classes that rely primarily on lectures and videos. Often during a biology lecture, Teresa will become lost and ask me, "What is he talking about?" When I suggest that she raise her hand and ask the teacher to explain the point again, she shakes her head, "No." She is embarrassed to draw attention to her lack of understanding. The few times she does ask for clarification in her English and science classes, the teachers' explanations only confuse her further and increase her reluctance to ask for help. For instance, she becomes frustrated while watching a video of *Death of a Salesman* in English class. She asks the teacher, "What's going on now?" He tells the class, "It's a flashback to his past." Teresa nods her head but is still confused. Later she complains to me: "The teacher wants us to watch the movie to understand the book better, but that's not working. The movie goes too quick." She prefers to read the play at home where she can look up terms in her Spanish/English dictionary or ask her uncle (when he is in town) to help her translate the "big words."

Teresa also becomes upset when she fails to understand humorous moments in class. Many times during the semester, a teacher made a joke or a student said something under his or her breath to cause the other students to laugh. Teresa, who often failed to understand the wisecracks, would ask: "What's so funny?" When I repeated the jokes to her verbatim, she usually replied: "I don't get it," and by the time I tried to explain the pun, the humor was often lost in the translation. These moments, though not necessarily connected to her academic achievement in school, serve to remind Teresa that she is still, in her words, a "weirdo" who cannot truly reach her goals until she speaks and understands English "perfectly."

TERESA
GOMEZ

Teresa's written work is another source of frustration. She makes numerous spelling and subject-verb agreement errors that her English and history teachers circle in bold red pen marks. She moans out loud when she gets an essay back in class and realizes how many corrections she must make. "Aaay. My [English] teacher won't put a grade on it until it is perfect," she complains,

> I want my writing to improve this year, but I want to learn like how to structure essay or to write good introductions. He just says, "Here's a list of topics," like "how dogs make better pets than cats" or "tell what is in your room at your house," and then like marks all our mistakes. I'm not learning how to write such a good report.

Though she corrects the circled errors on her English essays, and is clearly upset by how many errors she makes, Teresa is more upset about the quality of her writing instruction. She feels that her English teacher "is not doing a good job," and this feeling grows stronger as the semester progresses.

She makes similar complaints about her science teacher:

TERESA
GOMEZ

He is not very good because he doesn't explain things and just says "read the book." He also tests us on all these little details and makes the question, like, tricky. Like, this is how I study: I write down a thing like acid or base, and then I try to write out a sentence of what it is. But when I am studying I get, like, really very nervous, and then I get a stomachache, and I get so I can't study no more. I try to say to myself, "This is not a test—just review," but it hurts and then I can't concentrate. Then when I get to the test, I fail because I haven't studied! I can't remember anything. I just am blank and can't think.

I witness this kind of test "anxiety" on several occasions. Teresa wrinkles her brow, she pounds her head with her fist, she moans, she stares at the ceiling. She scribbles some answers in desperation at the last minute and shakes her head—another bad grade. Afterward, Teresa blames the teachers for not teaching her well. She blames herself for not studying and for not knowing some of the words. She blames her runny nose and her lack of sleep. "I can't concentrate on anything these days. . . . I just don't know what is wrong with me."

Even in subjects where she feels fairly competent such as math or computers, Teresa struggles with the exams. Halfway through a test on writing business memos in her business computing course, Teresa panics. She cannot get the graph program to work. With only five minutes left in the period, she tries every possible means to run the program correctly, and after madly pressing various key combinations, she manages to print a small section of the required graph. I ask Teresa, "What happened? Was it really hard?" She shakes her head:

No. I knew the stuff. It wasn't hard at all, but I had to go the bathroom really bad. I thought I was going to die, so I couldn't concentrate on the computer . . . and it was so hot in the room. Ugh! And my mom won't let me cut my hair even though it makes me so hot. She says, as long as I am living under her roof, I can't cut my hair—even though I say it will grow back! And then I know this bathroom is always broke, so I won't have time to go to the other bathroom, and like the timing is important because we fail if we don't finish on time. So aaaagh [she groans].

I sympathize with Teresa. Her thick hair hangs well below her waist and makes me sweat just looking at it. In addition, the trailer where this class takes place does get unbearably hot, and the nearest bathrooms *have* been broken for months. Perhaps another student would have asked for a few extra minutes on the exam, would have explained her situation to the teacher. Perhaps a less respectful daughter would have cut her hair despite her mother's wishes. But not Teresa. Unlike the giggling, excited student in the dance class, able to laugh at her mistakes and try the steps again, the "Teresa" we see in these classes appears to be anxious, shy, and lacking confidence. She is afraid to ask questions, she has trouble concentrating, and she feels isolated from her teachers and fellow students. "If only my English was better . . . " she says, without finishing the sentence. She puts much of the blame for her school frustration on her poor linguistic abilities, though it becomes clear (to both me and her) that her difficulty with English is only a part of the problem.

Eventually, as we spend more time together, Teresa reveals deeper sources for her frustration at school. She admits that "many things at Faircrest make [her] upset," so much so that sometimes the quiet, shy student feels compelled to speak out. She says: "Sometimes . . . I'm like a totally different person. . . . I do things

TERESA
GOMEZ

sometimes because I am so mad and because I want, like, the program to be better, and so we could learn more." This vocal and more assertive side often emerges when Teresa believes people are acting "unfairly"—when she believes students shirk responsibilities or when teachers fail to teach challenging and exciting lessons. As important to Teresa as perfecting her English is her desire to be "challenged" in school, and this desire leads her to make several important decisions during the semester, decisions that ultimately distinguish her from her peers and help her to acquire a reputation as an "outstanding student."

THE DESIRE TO BE "CHALLENGED"

Teresa originally decided to transfer into the business theme house because she was frustrated with her classes the year before. She thought they were "very easy and boring." The new theme house appealed to her because of its business and technology focus and because the students were often allowed to choose their own research topics. However, Teresa soon grew frustrated with these classes too. She complained about the quality of teaching in the three core classes, and she had little patience for the "immature" behavior regularly displayed by several of the business students. One group of boys in particular was extremely unruly. They made inappropriate comments and rude noises, and, on at least two occasions, pulled down their pants and "mooned" the other students during class. The first time this occurred, Teresa and a few other girls complained to their English teacher (who had not seen the incident), and the boys were told to "cut it out." The second time the boys pulled down their pants, the business computing teacher, a young woman who was new to the school, gave a similar warning and Teresa rolled her eyes: "You see what I mean? They are so immature, and the teachers can't control them."

In January, when Teresa's former English teacher, Ms. Dixon, passed her in the hallway and asked how she liked the new program, Teresa decided to tell the truth. She said she was frustrated by some of the teachers, especially her current English teacher. He wasn't really teaching her how to write, and he let the class take advantage of him. He was, in Teresa's terms, "very, very old and deaf" (he was in his late fifties), and he couldn't "control the noisy boys" and didn't "get them excited to learn." "He talks in a very boring voice, and he doesn't know how to make it fun for us," she continued. Ms. Dixon was concerned, and because the Business House was only in its first year, she suggested that Teresa share her complaints about the program with the school principal.

TERESA GOMEZ

At first Teresa refused. She had never spoken to the principal, Dr. Gold, before and was afraid to approach him with a complaint. Ms. Dixon suggested that she go with a group of her friends, but when Teresa tried to encourage several other students to join her, they also refused. They said it would be "too embarrassing," and they didn't want "to get involved." Finally, Teresa asked Ms. Dixon if she would join her in speaking to Dr. Gold. Together, they set up an appointment and discussed "the discipline problems in the class" and "how the classes weren't challenging." The principal promised to talk to the teachers and told Teresa to see him again if "things [didn't] seem to change."

For students who regularly and purposely interact with administrators and teachers, such as Kevin and Eve, meeting with the principal may not be such a fearful experience, but students like Teresa and her friends usually try to avoid contact with school officials. They rarely set foot in the main building for reasons other than obtaining tardy slips and schedule changes, and they view most administrators as disciplinarians ("people you see when you are in trouble"). Thus, when Teresa reflected on her decision to meet with Dr. Gold, she said she was "proud" that she went, especially given her "shyness." She admits that she would never have pursued such a meeting if she didn't feel strongly about some of the problems that were occurring, and she was glad that she "at least tried to make the program better." She was quick to mention, however, that she did not plan to meet with the principal again because "he did no good really."

A month after the meeting, Teresa, still frustrated with the lack of class control and the "easy assignments," complained to me that she was "not being challenged, not working hard because you don't *have* to study." She noted that she was still very busy, especially with her non-business courses like biology and Spanish and her family and work obligations, but that her Business House teachers didn't "push" the students. The pace of the classes was agonizingly slow for Teresa. For example, in English class, students spent more than two months reading and watching the movie *Death of a Salesman* and passing many hours in the computer room supposedly working on various short essays (though most of this time was spent chatting and complaining about the heat). Computer class felt even slower as the students had to wait for the teacher to check each individual screen during lessons on using new programs. Teresa usually finished the daily assignments in less than ten minutes and then "played" on the Internet until the teacher completed her rounds. Bored and frustrated, she sometimes put her head down on the desk and took a short nap.

In history class, the students had only two assignments for the entire semester, as the teacher wanted to give them the opportunity to focus "in-depth" and to become "experts" on certain topics. Teresa criticizes this approach: "We don't have any quizzes or tests in history; only the two big reports are graded, and we either do library, computer room, or movies . . . so we're not really learning history." Though she liked the freedom to choose her own report topics,[3] Teresa thought it was "strange" that her only knowledge of U.S. history this semester came from watching various World War II videos and listening to students' brief, disconnected reports on such topics as varied as the history of the automobile or the life of Lucille Ball. She wonders why the teacher didn't hold the students accountable for learning the information presented in the movies and reports and takes this as a sign that the information "wasn't important or we would be quizzed." Though she appreciated that this was the only course of the three in the Business House that seemed "different" in both content and structure from a course offered in the traditional high school curriculum, she worried that she was missing out on "basic events and information" that she wanted to know. For instance, after watching two fairly graphic films on the Holocaust, Teresa, visibly upset by the violence, asked me, "Why was everyone killing all the Jews? This is the first time I have heard of this."[4]

TERESA
GOMEZ

In addition to her frustration over the pace and structure of the courses, Teresa was angry with some of her teachers for not "treating the students fairly." In fact, she surprised the teachers and students on a few occasions by speaking her mind about what she felt were inappropriate and unfair actions. For example, early in the semester when a group of students told the history teacher that they were not yet ready to present their oral report, Teresa yelled out, "Give them an F, Mr. Grady, they had more than enough time!" She was upset because she and her partner worked through the night to get their report ready and would have benefited from having another day. She wanted the other students to be held to the same standard. The teacher raised his eyebrows at Teresa, then said to the group:

TERESA GOMEZ I am getting pressure here from the class. How would this fly in the world of work? We're trying to teach you priorities here. How 'bout we let the class make the decisions of what to do here? What is causing the delay?

One member of the group complained: "The printer messed up the report." "The printer is fine," snapped Teresa, "they're lying." Now some of the other students began to yell, "Yeah, they're liars, Mr. Grady." Teresa had sparked a class argument. "Give them an F," she continued, "they had plenty of time!" The teacher finally attempted to end the mayhem by conducting a class vote. Because only four students (out of 19 that day) agreed with Teresa that the students should fail, the group was allowed to present their report one day late with a half-grade penalty for the delay. After class, Teresa was still mad: "It's not fair. They should fail."

She used this same angry tone later in the semester when discussing her second group report in history class on the conflict in Rwanda:

Our group was so disorganized, and they said we would meet, but we never would. I was so mad at Carla [a friend in her group] because we were supposed to get together to work on the report, and then she left the library and took the report with her. Then I went to her house, and she said she didn't have the report, said she gave it to Jesus [another student]. And so I was so mad. And I got so mad and before I went to her house, I went and talked to Mr. Grady and said, "Mr. Grady, she was supposed to wait for me and she didn't and I'm tired of doing all the work and I'm tired of telling them what to do."

Once I told Jesus to do examples of conflict and so he say, "I did it, I did it, but I forgot" like for four days, "Oh, I forgot, I forgot, but I did it." And then the last day I got mad 'cause he didn't bring them so I realized that he *didn't* do it so *I* start to do it.

They're like, what's that called, when you . . . um, they're like, um, expecting me to do like everything like, or they know that if they don't do anything, I will do the work and like leaning on me. That's what I told Mr. Grady 'cause it's not fair that they're going to get an A or a B without doing anything.

And I don't think my report is that kind of, that good 'cause if all of us, the three of us would have worked together, maybe we could have done something good 'cause it's, um, I haven't had time like to, like three hours or four hours and I have to sit and do the whole . . . all the report or, 'cause I have other homeworks and so I don't think it's going to be that good.

On the day of the Rwanda report presentation, Teresa did not want to speak in public, so she instructed Carla to read the paper aloud. Carla refused and did not stand up at the front of the class with Teresa and Jesus during the presentation. Mr. Grady asked, "Carla, aren't you part of this group?" Carla replied, "Yes, but Teresa wouldn't let me do anything. She wouldn't let me read the report or do anything for the project." Teresa fired back: "That's not true! *You* didn't want to read or do anything. Jesus and I did it all." After class, Teresa says about Carla: "She is mad that I said that in front of the class. She said I should have said it in a different way. Now she is not speaking to me. But I told the truth." Later she found out that she received an A on the paper, Jesus earned a B, and Carla got a C. She was glad that Mr. Grady listened to her complaints and awarded the grades "fairly."

In each of these instances, Teresa felt like she "just had to say something." Despite her shyness and difficulties with English, Teresa made the decision to speak out against "things that [weren't] right" or "fair" in her eyes. She felt strongly that "everyone do their job" in school: teachers should maintain class control and design interesting and challenging lessons for their students; in turn, students should treat their teachers and peers with respect and strive to meet deadlines on time and fulfill group work obligations. Moreover, if the Business House was supposed to prepare students for future careers, then, according to Teresa, they had better start holding students accountable for their actions and start teaching "more information that will be useful in the real world." This year she had wanted to improve her writing and speaking skills, learn "more advanced computer skills," and practice using multimedia technology when giving reports, and though she was doing some of this in her business courses, she felt that "it was sort of a wasted year" and that she could have been learning "much, much more." By May, Teresa was seriously considering dropping out of the Business House for the following year. She had tried to help "make the program better" by talking to the principal and her history teacher, but at this point she "didn't think [the program was] going anywhere."

Ironically, about the same time that Teresa decided the year had been "a waste," she received a letter in the mail inviting her to attend the student recognition night, a time for all "outstanding students" to be formally recognized by their teachers. She was genuinely surprised by the invitation:

> When I first got it in the mail, I said, "ME?" I was very surprised. Why me? Mr. Grady asked if I was going. He said I should go and, um, that he would explain more to me later. Lucinda [a Mexican friend of Teresa's who took mostly honors level courses] got one too. She says she is not going. She says you have to sit sep-

arate from all the people who don't get the awards, and you stare at all the white kids, and, like, there are like no Mexicans up there and so you feel really stupid. All the white kids hang out together there, you know. . . . I think I may have to work that night; we'll see.

TERESA
GOMEZ

A week later we talk about the night. Teresa did not attend. Mr. Grady picked up the award on her behalf. I ask her what the award certificate said specifically, and she turns red with embarrassment. Looking down at the ground she whispers: "Um. I think it was for outstanding Business House student." I am happy for her and want to hear more: "Congratulations! Have you told anyone? Did you tell your mom?" Still looking down, she replies, "Yeah. Only two people got the award I guess, so she was all excited. She said she's gonna frame it and hang it in my room." I ask, "Are you proud of this?" Teresa sighs, "Not really." She explains:

> It's pretty easy to be in the Business House, and it's kind of like, yeah, I got all A's, but it should have been more difficult, then I would be proud of it, like oh, I did a good job. . . . It's like I didn't really deserve them [the good grades]. I didn't work hard. I am not proud of myself. Next year I want to work hard and get a 4.0. It will be hard, but I want to deserve it. That's why I didn't go to the awards dinner. I was kind of embarrassed. I could have got out of work if I wanted.

Here again, Teresa refers to an image of the way school ought to be. She believes school should be a place where one must *earn* good grades and deserve the awards she receives. Just as it isn't "fair" for Carla to receive an A on the Rwanda report without doing her share of the work, Teresa believes it isn't fair to accept the outstanding business student award without "working hard" for the honor. She wants to be challenged and engaged with her classes, she wants to feel worthy of her grades and honors, and she wants to be proud of the way she conducts herself with her teachers and peers. When compared to many of the rude and disorderly students in the Business House, and the students who regularly fail to meet deadlines or turn in homework, Teresa may appear to be "outstanding;" after all, she is fairly quiet and almost always hands in her work on time. However, Teresa is not interested in being compared to these peers; she wants to be recognized for doing excellent work, not for merely meeting course requirements.

It is this desire to learn and to work hard for her goals that may actually distinguish Teresa from her classmates and even set her apart from students like Kevin and Eve, who admittedly labor for their accomplishments but would never turn down an honor such as this. Whereas Kevin and Eve spend most of their school experience devising strategies to obtain good grades and titles by "all means possible," regardless of the actual learning they do, Teresa searches for a school program where it will be "difficult" to do well and where she believes she will therefore be motivated to study hard and learn the material. Teresa could have created her own challenging learning opportunities in her business classes. She could have pushed herself to write excellent reports and to do more than the minimum requirements, but she was ill most of the year, she had family commitments, she worked at the restaurant, and she was tired. She explained that she just wasn't motivated to work hard when she knew she "didn't have to."

Of course, wanting to behave in a certain way and actually fulfilling those expectations are two very different matters. When some of Teresa's non-business courses such as biology and algebra become increasingly difficult, for example, she panics. Instead of working hard to meet the challenges and becoming more moti-

vated to learn the material, Teresa resorts to "desperate" behavior. She cheats and commits plagiarism in order to salvage her
grades. These actions cause her to feel conflicted because, on the
one hand, she wants to "concentrate on learning" and not worry
about the grades, but she also wants to "do well to go to college,"
and she believes the C's and D's she is earning will hurt her chances.

THE DESIRE TO GO TO COLLEGE

Although Teresa's desire to be "challenged" and "pushed" to work
hard may distinguish her from her peers and from students such as
Kevin and Eve, her desire to go to college ultimately leads her to behave in similar ways to the grade-driven students. Like Kevin and
Eve, Teresa speaks in terms of compromising her beliefs and acting
in ways that do not make her proud. If she cannot be engaged with
all her courses, at the very least, she attempts to maintain grades
that will not prevent her from reaching another one of her goals.
As she explains:

> I cheated on like three or four bio tests this year, like 'cause, um,
> my uncle went back to Mexico and can't help me, and see my
> grades went down. . . . I also copy math homework a lot because
> you get points for turning it in. I, um, know it's not good and I
> shouldn't do it. I wish I could *not* do it, but, like, [pause] I want
> a future.

I ask if she thinks she will cheat again and, like Kevin, she nods her
head, "For when I don't study, and, and I still want a good grade. I
get scared so I bring in a [cheat] sheet. I don't like it, but . . . [She
shrugs her shoulders.]"

Often, Teresa plans elaborate cheating strategies with her friends,
sneaking off to the bathroom to devise the hand signals (one finger
flat on the desk means choose answer A, etc.) and scheming to-

gether to take the make-up tests during seventh period when the teachers are usually too busy talking in the resource room to notice any dishonest behavior from the students taking exams there. Usually, though, the cheating proves unfruitful, as her friends are almost as unprepared as she. She admits that her cheat sheets are written in such small print that they are sometimes of no use to her. Thus, despite Teresa's attempts to subvert the system, she still receives lower grades than she feels she needs, and she worries that next year she must do really well in order to be accepted to a state college. She is frustrated both because she believes she must break the rules to try to succeed in school and because this behavior "doesn't even help" her get the grades she desires.

This conflict is especially evident in Spanish class where Teresa receives her lowest grade ever for the semester, a D+. She giggles nervously and says her mother doesn't understand how she can be getting such a low grade in the class where she already speaks the language, but Teresa blames it on missing so many days and never paying attention. Instead, she does most of her algebra and biology homework during her Spanish lessons. Though other students (mostly non-native Spanish speakers) are routinely asked to put away textbooks from other classes, Teresa and a few of her peers are openly allowed to work on other subjects during class time. When I ask about this special treatment, Teresa replies:

> The teacher only cares about four people in the class, and they are all white. Ricardo agrees. He says Ms. P is racist against Mexicans. It's because she is from Cuba. [Teresa smiles.] No, just kidding, that's racist too! But she only really calls on those. The white kids have to do orals all the time too, but we don't, so it's kind of boring.

Throughout the semester I notice that only a handful of students
(mostly "white") are regularly included in the Spanish drills.

Throughout the semester I notice that only a handful of students (mostly "white") are regularly included in the Spanish drills. TERESA GOMEZ
Teresa rarely gets called on to participate in class, and Ricardo
manages to read *Animal Farm* day after day at his desk without
ever being acknowledged. Teresa knows she should study more and
pay attention to the lessons, but she feels as though the teacher has
little interest in her and, besides, she needs the time to finish her
other homework assignments. It seems that Teresa and Ms. P (along
with a few other native Spanish speakers) had established an un-
spoken "treaty" (Sizer, 1984; Powell, Farrar, and Cohen, 1985) of
non-interference: don't bother us, and we won't bother you. As
long as Teresa worked quietly at her desk on her math or science
assignments and demanded nothing from Ms. P, the teacher would
not call on her or ask her to put her other work away.

As the end of the semester drew near, Teresa decided, in effect,
to violate the treaty. She was determined to make up an important
test she had missed earlier in the week. Ms. P refused; "No, there is
not enough time left in the period." A few minutes later, Teresa
walked up to the teacher's desk and grabbed a copy of the test, ignoring the teacher's reply. When the teacher finally noticed that
Teresa had the exam and had begun filling in answers, she waved
her hand and sighed, "Oh, OK. Take the test. You can always finish
tomorrow." Teresa smiled, pleased with her small victory, but she
immediately moaned when she saw some of the difficult exam
questions.

The following week, Teresa whispered to me that she was going
to "do a bad thing." In addition to the family-related tardies and absences that her mother called in to excuse, Teresa had accumulated
many unexcused tardy marks in Spanish class from oversleeping
and from ditching on test days. In fact, she had so many tardies that

she worried she was in danger of being dropped from the class. She waited for the teacher to work with a group of students on the other side of the room, then cautiously crept over to the desk, found the attendance book, and erased several tardy marks from the ledger. She returned to her seat, smiling guiltily, then shrugged her shoulders and said:

> Oh, God, I try to be on time but the stupid light at the corner is so long, and then there is the long line of cars to get into the parking lot. . . . [I nod. I too have been caught in that line and have had to sprint to class.] My mom gets me out of Saturday school but not when they will drop you from a class. She gets mad and lectures me but I never have to go on Saturday.[5]

Teresa does not realize that she will never be dropped from a class as long as her mother "gets her out" of Saturday school. Only students who fail to attend their required number of Saturdays are expelled from certain courses, so Teresa commits the bold act for naught. Nevertheless, she feels uneasy about her decision to erase the tardy marks. She tells me later that the school is "right" to enforce the policy on tardiness and that it is "a good rule," but, similar to her view on cheating, Teresa feels compelled to take the risk in erasing the marks. She knows she should be on time; she knows she should not have to resort to cheating and other dishonest behavior to do well in school. She says she doesn't like to do these things but chooses to do them anyway because she believes her college career depends on it.

Interestingly, Teresa does not learn that one of her typical, time-saving procedures is considered "cheating" until a friend and I point it out to her. She boasts that she is writing her final English paper on Cesar Chavez, a hero of hers, because she had written an "A report" on him in middle school and still has the paper and all the same posters for the oral presentation. Her friend Lucinda, an honors track student, explains that using this report is technically cheating because Teresa never cites her sources in the paper: "It's like the same as copying the words from a book." Teresa looks surprised and asks me to verify this. I explain the concept of plagiarism but she is still not convinced. She asks:

TERESA
GOMEZ

> In college do they get mad or even know if you like copy what it says in the book for your reports? . . . But how will they know, especially if we change it into our own words? I mean, we probably do half our words and half the book's words—but we still have to understand it. I think that is OK still, don't you?

When I shake my head she looks shocked: "But everyone copies the book. They don't teach us that [referring to plagiarism] in my classes."[6] And though Teresa notes that this ignorance of academic convention represents yet another example of how the Business House is not preparing students well for the future, she decides to use the middle school report on Chavez despite our warnings. It is, after all, the final and most important paper for the semester, and she does not have time to research and write another report.

Just as Teresa's strong outbursts in history class seem to clash with her usually shy and quiet persona, these cheating incidents seem to contradict her beliefs about fairness and deserving the honors she receives. She recognizes the contradictions, and even though she is not certain that she wants to attend college, she feels obligated to at least keep her options open. She sees a connection between going to college and becoming an accountant and earning "lots of money." She has been steered toward "college preparatory" classes by her counselors at school. Her mother has urged her to think about college. Even her boss at the restaurant has lectured her on the importance of further schooling. Teresa wants to concentrate on learning and being challenged, she wants to act in a way that seems "right" and "fair," but she also "wants a future," and, given her home and work schedules, her frequent illnesses, her teachers and classes, the prevailing emphasis on college admissions requirements, and a host of other factors beyond Teresa's control, these multiple desires seem at odds with one another. Even when she attempts to change certain factors, when she speaks out in history, visits the principal, skips the awards ceremony, for example, she finds her efforts fruitless. She cannot "make the program better" and she eventually gives up, resolving to search elsewhere for a challenging curriculum.

In May she asks a friend about a special four-hour-a-day course offered at the school called The Community Project (TCP) where students design group projects around central themes they choose each semester.[7] The friend highly recommended the program because of the "great friendships" she made with all kinds of students and because the students "had lots of say over what they were learning." At this point in the year, after feeling neglected by some of the older girls in her dance class, Teresa longed to make "real friends at school with people besides the Mexicans." She did not like how "separate" the students were at Faircrest. She also thought she might like working on large group projects with students who would do their share of the work, but she struggled with the decision to join the class because she didn't want to "make another mistake" by switching into a program that would disappoint her:

> Oh, God, I don't know what to do. I like to work on projects with lots of time. I like to do what I feel is important, so I may do TCP, but do you think the colleges think that looks OK? I don't know what to do. . . . I hate when I have to make big decisions. I just need to know how the colleges feel about it and how it looks on

your transcript, because I can get good grades in Business
House because it is easy, but I want to learn more. . . . I want
to go to a state college, so I want to ask if Community can
count for some of the required subjects [the colleges] have.

In addition to worrying about college admissions criteria, Teresa
worries about the kinds of students enrolled in the class, and this
concern sparks a discussion on stereotypes and class differences, a
topic upon which, up until this point in the school year, Teresa had
declined to elaborate:

> Some friends of mine say that only gays and lesbians are in TCP.
> It's not true, right? I know it's not true, but, oooh, I don't know
> if I should apply or not. They also say that Business House stu-
> dents are weird, and that, well . . . that they are um, dumb. And
> I say, well at least I am not weird. I mean I may be the only nor-
> mal person in here [she looks around the room]. I mean . . .
> business classes are really easy and people *still* don't do well.

> I think everyone is disappointed with this program. I don't think
> it will be here after next year. . . . 'Cause I don't think they've
> put a lot of effort in this program 'cause you know how rich
> people . . . are like supporting the school, so they want more of
> their kids to go to college, . . . and this program it, like, has only
> people from downtown [a neighborhood she does not consider
> to be wealthy], and I think the rich people are supporting the
> school, and 'cause you know how a lot of Latino people come
> over here, and their parents, they don't have, like, good jobs like
> these people do, so they pay, like, small amount of taxes or
> small amount and, I don't know, I think that's why.

I ask, "Do you think the rich students get treated differently here?"
Teresa replies:

TERESA
GOMEZ

I think that the parents from [the wealthy neighborhood] don't like it, don't care about the business program which, would it be for just, I'd say for white people, it would be totally different.

Just as Teresa holds strong opinions about the way school ought to be, she holds strong beliefs about the way school "is." This conversation, as well as her references above to the white and Mexican students at awards night, and her comment that the Spanish teacher is "racist," reveal that Teresa perceives a difference in the way the white and Mexican students are treated at school. She associates qualities such as whiteness, wealth and power (at least power over the school curriculum) with the students who live in the suburbs. She sees some sort of connection between the amount of taxes one pays and an ability to influence school decisions such as who teaches and what material is taught in school programs. She is convinced that the honors program and other programs where "white" students are well represented are "better" because "white parents" want to ensure that their kids get into college and will "make sure" the program is "good."[8]

When we discuss her own parents' beliefs about college, Teresa admits that her mother would like her to go. She says her mother used to "pressure [her] to finish homework and get good grades— or she wouldn't take me to Mexico in the summers." Now that Teresa is in high school, she says her mother rarely pressures her (aside from a comment now and then on her Spanish grade):

> She cares about my grades, but she's not like "Oh, you have to get an A, you have to get an A." She says . . . "if you don't care about your grades, you're the one that's going to suffer the consequences in the future—so if you don't want to do your homework, or if you don't want to be responsible . . . you're the one that's left with the consequences."

'Cause I think she knows that I will do the work and I am responsible, and I think I want to go to college, but right now
that's the issue 'cause like I am scared that I am not going to
be able to go to college because of the money, so I'm like, ohhh
[she puts her head in her hands].

Teresa thinks she is different from her Mexican friends who may
not want to go to college because her mother encouraged her early
on and taught her to think about the future. She adds:

I think it has to be a lot of the way you're raised and like your
family, that kind of thing. I don't say that I'm mature, but my
friends they are not mature and don't think ahead. . . . They
don't want a future. Maybe I am more mature because I am the
only one at home with no brothers or sisters.

It is this sense of "future" that finally helps Teresa decide to apply
to The Community Project. She hopes the course will help her to
"make closer friends, be less shy, learn better English," and that it
will "challenge" her and "make [her] learn more" so that, in the future, she can go to college (if she figures out how to pay for it) and
get a "high paying job." And though she still worries that colleges
will not "like" her decision to switch into such a non-traditional
course, she feels better when she realizes she "can always drop out"
if the program does not meet her expectations (regardless of what
the colleges might think of that). Even after supposedly resolving
to join TCP, however, Teresa has a moment of doubt and skips her
obligatory interview with the teacher. Only after Teresa convinces
her dance teacher, who happens to be engaged to the Community
teacher, to intervene on her behalf, is she given a second chance to
interview for the course.

Such contradictory behavior is not surprising from a student who reveals so many different sides to herself, and it becomes clear to me that few people have a sense of the complexity of Teresa's life. Some teachers know that she works and that she has many home responsibilities, but few know just how much she does in a day and the toll these responsibilities take on her school work. Some see only her shy side and express surprise when she complains; others, like the counselor who recommended her for the study, see a student who is committed to academics and takes steps to improve her school experience. Some see a student who gets straight A's in the Business House and is named "outstanding," while some, like her Spanish and science teachers, see a student with frequent absenteeism struggling to get a passing grade. Few hear her views on being challenged and motivated; even fewer hear her worries about college and the future. Through it all Teresa manages to cling to her dream of wanting more out of school, enough so to speak out at times and search for "greener pastures." Though she does not see the connection between what she is doing in dance class and what she wants from her academic subjects, it seems clear that she searches for a venue where she feels comfortable enough to speak freely and laugh at her mistakes and motivated enough to want to take the music home and practice her steps until they are perfect.

CHAPTER 5

Michelle Spence:
Keeping Curiosity Alive?

Sitting near the top of the bleachers in front of an empty football field on a cool March afternoon, Michelle Spence plays with the strings on the torn edges of her faded bell-bottom jeans. Pushing her long, honey colored hair out of her face, she smiles as she recalls the "family atmosphere" at the small private school she attended from third to eighth grade:

> There were only about 17 students in each grade, and we called all the teachers by their first names, and they treated you as people. . . . And it was just like a big group of friends that were just learning something, and if you got something wrong it wasn't bad, you just did it again and got it right. And people were at all different levels, and they weren't sectioned off into different classes. We all took the same class and it was, if someone was a little behind, they'd just help them individually, you know, just nudge them along. . . .

MICHELLE
SPENCE

And they had the equivalent of three periods a day where we could weave, do art, cook, go do science, music, clay, you name it, during the free periods. You could do all this stuff on your own. In six hours of school, you had half the time to explore and do all this stuff. . . . You could let your imagination run wild.

I think why I loved it is that it's like, it wasn't a pressure learning system where you know you have to learn. Like, that entire system was sooo much looser than this [the high school]. We'd go on camping trips all the time, go on field trips. And even though [it was] so much looser and, you know, laid back than it is here, it worked 100 times better because everyone wanted to come to school, and everyone wanted to do what we were doing. . . . Learning was so much fun there, you didn't even know you were learning. It just sort of happened.

For Michelle, the small, personal, discovery-oriented environment of her elementary school where "you didn't even know you were learning" represents an "ideal" far removed from her first few years in high school. She describes the transition from Horizons Elementary to Faircrest High as "extremely frightening." She felt lost at the large public school without her close friends and worried that she would not be able to keep up with the other students. Having never been given grades before, she felt "stressed about getting A's" and "pressured by the whole set-up" to succeed:

You feel like oh if you don't get good grades, you won't go to college and all this bad stuff will happen to you—you're bad, you're stupid, that type of stuff. It just feels like if you don't get the good grades then you won't succeed in society. And . . . being a perfectionist, I could not allow myself to get anything lower than A's, 'cause I knew I was an A potential person . . . I just, I was al-

ways like oh I got to get an A, I have to get an A on this test,
have to do all my homework, have to do everything, and I just
got so overloaded.

MICHELLE
SPENCE

She regretted feeling the need to compete with the other students for the high grades and believed that many of them resented her when she performed well on a test or answered questions correctly in class. She explains that she "made a few enemies" freshman year when she refused to give some students the answers to a math exam, and since then, she tried to hide her good grades from her peers. She resolved to "sit and listen quietly" and not ask too many questions in some of her classes where she might be considered a "know-it-all." She wasn't used to a system where students felt the need to cheat in order to get high grades, and she did not like hiding the fact that she was interested in the material and "really wanted to learn, to be interactive."

Halfway through her sophomore year, Michelle realized that she needed to make a change. She was taking seven classes, one of which was an honors course, and she had at least five hours of homework to do each night. She found herself "crying all the time from the stress of trying to accomplish everything," and she contemplated dropping out of school. Her sister, who was two years older, had dropped out of Faircrest early in her sophomore year, passed the GED exam, and was currently taking classes at the local community college. Michelle knew that her sister was happy with the decision to leave Faircrest but that she also regretted "missing out on the prom and other things associated with high school that people who have skipped it look back and wish they had done." Michelle wanted to be sure she was making the right choice and consulted her parents and a few of her teachers for advice. Her drama teacher eventually helped to convince her to stay.

Michelle "didn't even know Faircrest had a drama department" until the first quarter of her sophomore year. She had "always loved acting," doing "little class plays for the parents at Horizons Elementary—nothing professional, just a lot of fun." She tried out for a play at Faircrest early in her sophomore year and landed a small part. Ms. Fogarty, the new, young drama teacher, directed the play and noticed Michelle's talent. She told Michelle that she would most likely be cast in many more plays at the school, and that this was one reason to stay. She also told Michelle that the diversity of students at the high school provided an opportunity for learning how to "communicate with others" and for gaining "socialization skills," and that she "could learn a lot about society in a place like this."

Michelle thought her teacher's points were "very convincing," but added that her decision to stay in school was driven, in part, by fear. She was "scared and intimidated to make the wrong choice and regret it the rest of [her] life."

> I'm the type of person who tends to do something for a while, and, a lot of the time, if something's not giving satisfaction, I'll just drop it. Like horseback riding, I was getting really good, but then I just got bored with it and I stopped. And basketball, I got to varsity during freshman year, and I was just looking back on it today . . . and thinking, God, if I'd stayed I would have been incredible now. . . . So I decided to try this [new] class, and if that doesn't work, I said, "I am leaving."

Michelle's fear of making the wrong decision stemmed in part from her knowledge that she often stopped activities when she became bored and that she usually regretted her actions afterward. But the fear and intimidation she felt also resulted from the notion that success in high school was inextricably tied to success in life. Like

Kevin and Eve, Michelle felt tremendous pressure to get A's, to reach her "potential" and thereby secure a happy future. She felt overloaded and knew that she had to resist the system that caused her to feel this undue stress. She felt fortunate that the school offered The Community Project (TCP) which allowed her both to stay in high school and to opt out of a system that was making her so unhappy.

MICHELLE
SPENCE

Michelle was attracted to The Community Project for some of the same reasons Teresa was. She liked the idea of doing group projects, of working "*with* students instead of competing against them," and of being able to "design [her] own curriculum." Her sister had actually joined TCP in ninth grade, the year before she dropped out of school, so Michelle knew much about the program before she decided to apply. She knew TCP was small (limited to 25 students), that it met each day from 8 AM to noon, and that the teacher liked students to call him by his first name. She knew the course promoted "self-initiated learning" where each student was encouraged to pursue individual interests in addition to working on the class projects, and that it was not oriented around grades. Though the teacher, Richard, awarded each student a grade at the end of every quarter, he did so only after consulting with the students about the grades they felt they deserved. Aside from these quarterly grades, there was no other graded work in the course. When Michelle found out she had been accepted to the class for the following year, she was excited; TCP represented "the closest thing to Horizons" that the high school had to offer.

An Alternate Course

Richard developed The Community Project twenty years ago with the help of a small group of students, parents, and administrators who wanted a school that would "more effectively touch the essence

MICHELLE
SPENCE

of the learner." Based on the "spirit of Herb Kohl's open classroom" and on the "writings of Jonathan Kozol, George Brown,
and John Dewey," TCP, according to Richard, is not just a course
at Faircrest High, but an "alternative school unto itself," designed
to be:

> significantly different from the conventional school, . . . in terms
> of its freedom, sensitivity to emotion, methods of inquiry, ad-
> ministrative structure [the students share decision-making re-
> sponsibilities with Richard on everything from the curriculum
> to the course budget], and . . . how it approaches the whole phe-
> nomenon of change, growth, and transformation in the learner.[1]

As his language suggests, Richard is schooled in psychology, and
the one "required" aspect of TCP is that students "give" Richard
four hours each week to teach them "psychological systems." The
rest of the curriculum is "co-created" by Richard and the class. They
choose the themes they wish to study for the year; schedule the
various projects, student presentations, guest speakers, readings,
debates, and so on, to take place each month; lead the class sessions
(for example, pairs of students take charge of each activity during
the four-hour session, rather than having Richard head every project); and ultimately assess whether or not they have been successful in their pursuits. In addition, each student writes an independent study contract for projects to be done outside of class time. For
successfully participating in TCP, students receive school credit in
psychology, history, English, physical education, and environmen-
tal studies. Other science, language, and math classes can be taken
after fourth period, outside of TCP, in the conventional school.

Richard and the students worked hard to make their course
seem "totally different from regular classes at Faircrest." The class-

room itself was noticeably more comfortable and student-friendly. It was the only classroom I saw in the school with wall-to-wall carpeting which, aside from being more aesthetically appealing than linoleum, proved extremely useful for sitting on the floor during group work. The room had a piano, several computers and printers, a television and VCR, various throw rugs placed over the carpeting, a refrigerator (open to all students anytime during class when they wanted to eat or drink), several chairs, tables, and chalkboards, as well as two comfortable couches for lounging or even napping when a student felt ill.

MICHELLE SPENCE

Time spent in the classroom was also different from more conventional classes I observed, both because of the students' roles in curriculum design and implementation, as well as the wide variety of subjects addressed. In one week, for instance, students read and discussed the book *Flatlands,* debated censorship in schools, watched the film *The Color Purple,* studied Kohlberg's theory of moral development, listened to a guest speaker explain the workings of the Internet, learned to cook an authentic Mexican meal, discussed the recent events in the Middle East, made African masks from various natural materials, and held a community meeting to explore fundraising for a service project in a third world country. Each project was scheduled in one-, two-, or three-hour time slots, and though each related to one of the main themes selected in the beginning of the year, such as "cultural issues" or "tools of science," I noticed little sense of coherence between the various activities.

Once accepted in the program, Michelle attempted to prepare for the many different assignments during the week, going to the library late at night to find articles on censorship, reading newsmagazines for updates on the Middle East, and gathering the necessary materials from the International Development organization

MICHELLE
SPENCE

for the community meeting she was to lead, but she was busy with her other classes, math and drama, and with the Thespian Club and her singing groups. In the end she regretted that she knew "almost nothing about Israel" when she was supposed to discuss peace prospects and admitted that she "had to skimp" when preparing her statements for the school censorship debate. Even the community meeting felt rushed and unproductive, and Michelle worried that the class would never reach consensus on which international service project to sponsor.

At the time the meeting was supposed to begin, Richard happened to be out of the room. Michelle knew that the class only had one hour to discuss the project, so she quickly took charge. She quieted the students and divided them into four groups to read the service proposals. Each group was supposed to rank the proposals and reconvene in the large group for a final vote. After 20 minutes Michelle announced, "You have about ten minutes to wrap it up." Once in the large group, she discovered that one group had voted quite differently from the others. Continuing in the role of facilitator, she encouraged the group by saying: "Don't give in. Let's think about this. Should it be the maternity clinic at the school in Ghana or the fishery in [Nigeria]? What it comes down to is education, life, or food. What will this money really do?" Later when the class could not decide and some students wanted to split the money, Michelle stepped in again and argued against the split since she believed it would be "harder to fundraise for two separate projects." At the end of the allotted time, the class was still debating which project to do, and neither side showed signs of giving in.

This indecision troubled Michelle because she "really wanted the class to take on one big community project" in addition to the various small service projects they had planned for the year like tutoring in a local kindergarten and working with Habitat for Humanity. Describing herself as "a kind of activist," Michelle explained that she believed in "taking steps toward making a difference in the world;" for instance, she did not eat animal products of any kind (no meat, eggs, cheese, etc.) in order to support animal rights and protect the ecosystem, and she boycotted certain clothing stores such as the GAP "because what they do to their workers in East Asia is really horrible." She wanted to see the class raise the money for the service project by staging a "talent showcase extravaganza" at the high school and charging ten dollars a ticket for admission, but she was too busy with drama rehearsals every night and homework piling up to give this project the attention she felt it deserved.

MICHELLE SPENCE

Three weeks into the second semester Michelle realized that her school commitments were "taking a toll on [her] health." She had missed several days of school due to a series of colds, rousing herself out of bed to attend drama rehearsals each afternoon and then collapsing back into bed when she returned home at 9 PM. She felt that she hadn't "been taking care of [herself]" and "wasn't organizing [her] time well." Tests and projects were "coming in waves," and she hadn't prepared for things to "happen all at once." High tide hit just before she was supposed to leave for San Diego to perform in a statewide drama competition.

She needed to obtain Richard's permission to miss school for two days to attend the competition, but, according to Michelle, Richard didn't want her to go. He believed "drama was taking up too much of [her] time," and that she "wasn't honoring [her] commitment to come to class each day." Richard "accused" her of being "three weeks behind in [her] work for TCP," which Michelle denied. She told him she was only a few days behind due to her poor health and that she was catching up:

MICHELLE
SPENCE

I was like, "No, actually I'm not three weeks behind, more like three days. . . ." I mean he was trying, he knows where my sensitive spots are, and one of them is academics because that's really important to me. . . . And he kept saying, "Where's your commitment, Michelle?" and he got into this whole guilt trip type thing. I mean it was absolutely ridiculous. I felt almost like mentally, if not manipulated, then abused just by, like, I couldn't believe that he was being so stubborn and one-sided. I don't know, it was like he didn't expect me to want to do anything else except TCP, . . . and I was really upset because part of why I wanted to join TCP was to be able to be really involved in drama and get some credit [for reading plays and writing reviews, and so on] in TCP, and what's turning out happening is that like if you're in TCP, you can't have any other interests.

Richard finally allowed Michelle to go to the competition on the condition that she have a friend videotape the classes she would be missing. He was still upset, though, by the extent drama seemed to be interfering with his course and complained to both the drama teacher and the principal.

Michelle's frustration with TCP grew when Richard announced that all independent contract work needed to relate to the course themes for the year. Originally only group projects needed to be linked in some way to the themes students chose to study in September; now Richard wanted all the work students chose to do for credit in TCP to focus on the themes as well. He explained that he was worried that students had little opportunity to "go in depth" on any issues when they covered such a wide variety of topics each week. He hoped to streamline the course and encourage students to focus more intensely on fewer subjects. This change would prevent Michelle from getting credit for much of her drama work, as she would no longer be allowed to write essays analyzing her characters' behavior or create accurate accounts of the time periods in which the plays were set for U.S. history credit. She complained to me, "I came to TCP so I could do what I loved and get credit for it instead of do what someone else tells me to do and get credit for it, which is exactly what TCP is turning into." MICHELLE SPENCE

The class was allowed to vote on the proposed changes, but Richard was very persuasive in his arguments for the new system, and, as Michelle noted, "he's also the one who finally decides your grade, and I hate to say it, but some people have felt if they cross him, he will be hard on them." Hence, Richard's new system prevailed and, one month into the new semester, Michelle felt (once again) that she needed to make a change. TCP wasn't turning out to be anything like Horizons Elementary, and though she wanted to stay in school, she was not "willing to sacrifice [her] love for drama just because Richard felt [she] was unbalanced." Still, it was not easy to switch programs in the middle of a semester. Michelle had made a commitment to stay in TCP for the year and agonized over her decision to leave. Again she consulted her parents and drama teacher for advice. She worried that Richard might "sabotage [her] quarter grades" if he knew she was considering leaving TCP. Her school counselor suggested that she "make a fresh start" in some conventional courses and make up the four weeks of missed work rather than ask Richard to transfer her credit. Her drama teacher offered to teach an independent study course in American literature where Michelle could read several plays and write essays on topics of her choice. And her father assured her that her parents would support "whatever decision she made and help her with any make-up work."

Michelle finally opted to transfer out of TCP and into two classes in the "regular" school, U.S. history and psychology, along

MICHELLE
SPENCE

with the independent study English class with her drama teacher, Ms. Fogarty. Counting the math, drama, and music classes in which she was already enrolled, this meant that Michelle had six courses for the semester. Because the independent study class met only once a week, Michelle suddenly found herself with two free periods a day to make up the four weeks of work she had missed in history and psychology. The courses were "fairly easy," and she was able to catch up and get A grades for the quarter. Everyone seemed happy initially with the results, except for Richard.

When Richard discovered Michelle had received such high marks for the quarter, he called a meeting with the principal, Ms. Fogarty, and Michelle's counselor. Michelle was not invited; in fact, she didn't even know about the meeting until Ms. Fogarty told her what had taken place.[2] Apparently Richard was upset that Michelle had done "no work in his class for four weeks and was still able to get A's for the quarter." He said, "Obviously, she is trying to get away with something." He felt that Michelle should receive four weeks' worth of an F grade averaged with the grades she received in the remaining weeks of the quarter in her new courses. As Michelle related the story to me, she was extremely upset:

> Can you believe he wanted me to get an F? A zero! I mean he presented it as if I did absolutely no work for four weeks! . . . Even though I didn't ask for any credit for the work I did during that time, I *did* do work. So, like he lied, which is so frustrating for me because I wasn't there to defend myself. . . . And I can't believe he said I was trying to get away with something! Anyone who knows me, knows that is just not me. And he kept slicing me, making me out to be like a really sleazy like cheating, unresponsible person.

Michelle's father, too, was outraged at Richard's accusations. He called Michelle's counselor to "get the official story," and then called the principal to set up another meeting. There, according to Michelle, the counselor took her side immediately:

> He said, "Why are we bugging her? She's a successful student, and there's all these people who are failing, and you know, they're the people we should be paying attention to—not someone who's succeeding." And I was like yeah give me a break, exactly, you know, I'm not the one who needs attention in this type of matter, especially to take up the principal's time. Hello?

> And then my dad was concerned that Richard was like monitoring me and wanted to make sure he couldn't intervene anymore, and then he [the principal] did a little of his, you know, butt kissing to my dad like saying, "Oh she's a great student," and complimented me on my acting in the last two plays, and then he assured my dad that, you know, Richard won't be doing anything with me. But also what's going to happen is he's going to check into TCP. He said where he's going to talk to some students who are currently in there because I had told my dad and my dad told the principal that, you know, there's some people in there who would want to leave but they're afraid of what would happen. You know students are trapped in there.

As Michelle said this, I wondered if some of the other students actually felt "trapped" in TCP, or if she was being a bit overly dramatic in her account. I knew students who were thrilled with the alternative program and who believed the course "saved their lives." One student even returned to the school after dropping out in order to attend Richard's course. However, given the emphasis on community and commitment to the group, I could also see how students might feel they were letting the class down by opting to leave. Michelle felt some of this pressure, and she worried about "peer approval" of her decision but realized that she "would be really unhappy if [she] stayed."

Michelle was more fortunate than most students in that she had access to the right people and resources to help her carry out the decision to leave. She was highly visible in the school due to her drama activities, and the school counselor and principal had seen her in several performances. They considered her to be both a "great actress" and an "excellent student" with a nearly perfect grade point average, and they would see to it that she would not be hassled again. The drama teacher, Lisa Fogarty, also played a key role in Michelle's transition out of TCP. She served as Michelle's mentor and main source of support at the school. She consistently defended Michelle's actions and advised her on how to respond to Richard's accusations. In offering to teach an independent study English class, Ms. Fogarty made a personal sacrifice to take time out of her already overloaded schedule to help Michelle "get credit for doing something she loved"—reading and studying plays. She had helped to convince Michelle to stay in school before and knew the kind of freedom her star pupil desired.

Michelle's parents also provided encouragement and love, allowing her to make the decisions "herself" and assuring her that they would support whatever decisions she made. They knew when to intervene and take action on her behalf, skillfully navigating the school system, arranging a meeting with the principal to assure that their daughter would be treated fairly, and following up with phone calls of appreciation. Michelle was grateful for this help and especially praised her father's support. She spent most of her time with her father since her parents' divorce years ago. He was a pre-school director who lived with Michelle and her sister in an apartment

downtown. He also worked some evenings as a massage thera- MICHELLE
SPENCE
pist "to help make ends meet." Michelle's mother was a computer consultant for a law firm in a nearby city where Michelle
stayed once or twice a week, fighting thirty minutes of traffic to get
to school in time for first period. Both parents had been guest
speakers and visitors to TCP last semester and knew Richard well.
Both parents also attended all of Michelle's drama and music performances and knew how much she loved to perform. Unlike Kevin
and Eve, Michelle believed her parents would be supportive of her
decisions "no matter what." Whereas Kevin's sister who attended
community college was thought to have "really messed up her life,"
Michelle's sister who attended the same college was treated with respect, and Michelle knew she would be too. She credits her father
(and her early private school experience) for her "motivation to be
a self-initiated learner":

> I think my dad was the reason that I'm motivated just because
> my parents were big, are really intent on learning, and they've al-
> ways made sure that, you know, the stress wasn't get an A or we
> won't love you. It was always, "I don't care what you get." They
> don't care. What they care about is me learning stuff. And what
> they want me to be is a good person and not, I mean, the grades
> really don't matter. I mean they do but they won't tell me. You
> know that's not what they say. They're proud when I get it but
> it's not something that's like strict. I never had that whole thing
> where you have to finish your homework before you do your
> phone because I can do it on my own, and they know I push my-
> self enough anyway.

> And then Horizons had a large part of it 'cause I mean where I'm
> coming from learning is fun. So if you've had an experience in
> life where learning is boring, obviously you're not going to want

MICHELLE
SPENCE

to do it 'cause you've had so many years of that you just want to get out of there. But if you've been taught, if all your experiences with learning have been fun and productive, you're going to have a whole different feeling.

Unlike many students, Michelle was fortunate to have had a positive view of learning early on—a taste of what it feels like to be engaged with the material. She had hoped that TCP would offer her a similar experience and allow her the freedom to pursue interesting topics in an environment where grades were considered less important than student engagement and growth. When Richard decided to change the course, and when her acting pursuits caused her to miss several days of school due to field trips and illnesses from an exhausting rehearsal schedule, Michelle grew frustrated. She knew she didn't want to drop out of school, but she couldn't find a program that satisfied her. "Ideally," she would have preferred a "combination of TCP and regular school" that would have allowed her to act in the school plays and pursue other academic interests as well, but that was not an option. Recognizing the limits of the school's programs, Michelle reluctantly decided to give up some of the freedom she enjoyed in TCP to be able to remain active in the drama department, one of the few places she felt genuinely challenged by the material and where she was given the support and encouragement to pursue her interests.

As part of the transfer agreement, Michelle promised to make up four weeks' worth of work, and though her new teachers did not require her to do all of this, it was important for Michelle to feel that she wasn't "getting away" with anything. As she said earlier, she was "sensitive" about academics and wanted to deserve her grades and believe that she had fulfilled her teachers' expectations. She said that anyone who knows her knows that she wouldn't try to "cheat" in this way, and she was right. The school people who knew Michelle came to her defense. Her parents and drama teacher who spent considerable time with her, as well as the counselor and principal who knew her through her grades and drama performances, all helped her to make a fairly smooth transition. Had Michelle not been as visible at the school or as well-connected, or had she not had such high grades or savvy parents, she might not have fared as well.

MICHELLE
SPENCE

She felt she was lucky to have so many people on her side, and yet she was frustrated that she had to make such unsatisfying choices. Though Michelle's reputation and grade point average remained virtually unscathed after the transition out of TCP, she felt that she had clearly sacrificed some of her intellectual needs. None of the school programs seemed to be designed with a student like Michelle in mind, a student who sought freedom to satisfy her intellectual curiosity and who was not willing to endure the overbearing stress caused by the pressure to get high grades. Michelle felt forced to "choose drama over academics," and added as if trying to convince herself, "Sometimes it's better to be a little bored [in regular classes]" in order to be able to "do what you love."

"Sacrificing Academics"

At first, after leaving TCP and transferring into her U.S. history and psychology courses, Michelle enjoyed some of the extra time she gained with two free periods a day. She managed to help clean the house and do some shopping, talk with friends on the phone, see a few movies, spend time with her family—"regular human things" that she was too busy to do earlier. She found that making up four weeks' worth of work was really quite easy since the teachers didn't actually expect her to turn in all the homework from the past month. Her psychology teacher asked her to make up two tests,

MICHELLE
SPENCE

which required reading the necessary chapters in the textbook and memorizing xeroxed lecture notes. Michelle got 100 percent on both tests. She was interested in the subject and liked the teacher's funny anecdotes and "wacky discipline system" (anyone who broke a class rule had to "do 25 pushups right there on the floor"). The teacher primarily lectured the students, interspersing personal stories throughout, and each talk was accompanied by a lecture outline with blank spaces the students were supposed to fill in as they listened. Michelle was one of the few students I saw who took notes in addition to completing the required outline. She knew she wouldn't be tested on this extraneous material, but she was "really interested in knowing more about people and their personalities." Her desire to learn the material above and beyond the course requirements was striking, and when I asked about this, she reminded me, "I am a self-initiated learner."

Michelle claimed that her new history class was "the easiest class [she] ever had." She admitted that she probably should have been in the honors history class but she could not have possibly switched into the course this late in the quarter. She said the history teacher "is sweet and really wants the kids to learn, but she's definitely new." The teacher had difficulty controlling the rowdy group of students and had not yet figured out how to gauge her assignments for the heterogeneous group. For example, she handed back a batch of tests and said to the class:

Six A's, 7 F's, and a few B's and C's [Michelle received an A+]. This is the challenge in this class, how to challenge the A students without losing the F's—any suggestions?

Some students yell out, "We weren't ready for the test," "you rushed us through the review," "lose the essay or at least make it shorter." The teacher replies, "All right, no homework this week, just study for Friday's test." Michelle shakes her head and resolves to read the textbook chapters that aren't assigned because she is interested in learning about the 1920s for a play she wants to read. She likes the textbook because it "tries a new approach." It offers "pieces of literature like *Grapes of Wrath* in each section and has critical thinking exercises to challenge you as you go along."

MICHELLE
SPENCE

Michelle tries to participate fully in history class despite its limitations but is continually frustrated by the other students' lack of motivation. In a group assignment where students are asked to answer questions based on a textbook chapter on the New Deal, Michelle is the only one in her group who has brought the book to class, let alone read it. When she tries to help the group answer the questions, she is criticized by one member who complains, "We don't need more information on the CCC. We just have to copy the book; we don't have to be creative." Despite the complaints, Michelle's group finished a half an hour early thanks to her, whereas many of the other groups hadn't even started. Students were busy discussing the latest gossip, beeping their pagers, banging on the desks to get the teacher's attention, or simply sleeping, hunched over the now crumpled worksheets. When the bell rings, the teacher agrees to give the students more time tomorrow to finish the assignment. Michelle whispers to me as we leave the classroom, "Maybe the reason why I read the extra chapters in the book is because I feel like, oh my God, I'm not getting anything accomplished here."

On another day, Michelle is paired with a student who received 11 points out of a possible 50 on the last test. They are supposed to make a presentation based on the readings from the previous night's homework. Michelle's partner informs her that she has not read the chapter and that she hasn't done any of the reading since October, when she lost her book. Michelle prepared a detailed overhead with a summary of key points from the textbook and tells her

MICHELLE
SPENCE

partner, "That's OK, just go up there with me." Moments before they are called to the front of the room, however, her partner disappears to the bathroom for 25 minutes. Michelle presents the overhead by herself, expanding on each point to the frustration of the other students who demand, "Slow down!" "Tell us what to write down in our notes." "There's too much stuff there to copy! Shit, you weren't supposed to write a book!" Throughout the presentation the teacher pleads, "Be nice. . . . Listen to Michelle. . . . No swearing," but it is of no use. The rudeness continues throughout other students' presentations as well. Michelle takes notes quietly from the back of the room and tries to memorize her monologue from *Othello*.

Later she tells me she felt as if she was learning "bits and pieces about various time periods but never getting the full picture" in her history course. She knew the teacher "was really trying," but Michelle worried that so much was missing:

> It's not as much of a complete story. . . . I mean it's more like vacant history. It doesn't seem alive. I mean she tries . . . like when she was going to teach us something about like the 60s she dressed up in a little tie-dyed shirt and had, like, incense. It was so cute 'cause she tried so hard and you know she's just learning how to do, like, what she's doing, teaching. But she lets the kids run all over her because she doesn't know how to, you know, play them yet. . . .

As she discussed the significant problems of her history course, Michelle showed extreme compassion for the teacher and a keen ability to articulate some of the failings of the school system. She recognized that the teacher was inexperienced and the students were out of control in the history class but explained that she was frustrated and bored by some of her other courses as well. She longed for a more cohesive approach to teaching and learning and complained that "sticking 30 people in a class . . . and then try[ing] to teach them all the same way . . . when everyone learns differently . . . that's just not fair."

MICHELLE SPENCE

She wondered if she wouldn't be more stimulated in the honors classes, but worried that she would feel "overloaded again," like she did during her freshman and sophomore years. For example, even though she received an A in her honors geometry course last year, she said the class went too quickly for her and she was unfairly expected to understand difficult concepts "right away." Sometimes when she asked questions, the teacher would make her "feel stupid" by saying, "You don't know that? You should." Michelle thought the other students were "whiz kids" because they appeared to understand the material instantly, and she felt as if she was slowing down the entire class when she raised her hand for help. She also believed that many of these students "had no life" outside of their honors courses and that it would be difficult for them to be as involved in drama and music as she was. She said, echoing Kevin and Eve, "I think you need to find some middle ground between having a life, enriching your life, and going to school or studying." She believed the honors classes required "a lot more work" and proceeded at a faster pace than the other classes, but that they were not necessarily more "interesting or challenging," nor would they offer her the freedom to follow her intellectual curiosity. More of the same at a faster pace was not what she desired, especially if it meant cutting back on some of the things she loved to do.[3]

Like the other students in this study, Michelle developed specific strategies to cope with her growing frustration over her courses. For instance, at first she tried to convince herself that the slow pace of this year's math class allowed her to "really learn the stuff in deep, learn the process of algebra really well." But she soon grew tired and bored with the course. She finished assignments, quizzes, and tests much earlier than the other students and often used this time to memorize lines or work on other homework. She frequently chose not to go to the class because she "wouldn't be missing anything." She explained that neither the teacher nor her parents seemed to mind her absences:

> My parents don't care. They always sign for me or call in. I'm OK with skipping it. I mean I know the material, and I am not affecting anyone, and not really losing anything by not being there. I wouldn't do it if I was behind. . . . The teacher knows I am not slacking off so she lets me do it. . . . We have developed a trust. She lets me do what I need to do.

Similar to Teresa's treaty with her Spanish teacher, Michelle had established an agreement with her math teacher. She was allowed to use class time to work on other assignments or decide not to go to class when she felt she could use her time more wisely. She was also given the flexibility to turn in assignments late if she was too busy to get them done by their due dates. The teacher told me she knew Michelle was a "good kid" who would "keep her 4.0 average in the class," and because of this, she believed Michelle would never abuse the privileges she received. Whereas Teresa's treaty contributed to her low grades in the course, Michelle's bargain did not seem to affect her high marks and might have even helped them.[4] Though Michelle appreciated the teacher's understanding and liked the freedom she was given, she was still disappointed with the course. The high grades meant little to her. She said, "There's nothing to strive for really. I mean an A in there is like an empty reward. I love algebra [the subject], . . . but the class is boring." She then adds, trying to convince herself, "At least I am really getting it. I guess it is better to get it and be a little bored." The treaty she formed with the teacher may have made her daily life more bearable, but it did not help her find a meaningful way to pursue her interest in the subject. The math teacher was not solely to blame; the problem was larger than that. Very few of Michelle's courses helped her to explore topics in ways which excited and challenged her.

MICHELLE
SPENCE

Later in the semester Michelle began to worry. She told me she had a "freakout attack" one morning about her schedule:

> I thought . . . this is my least challenging year, and it's my most important year in terms of college transcripts and stuff. And I am really worried. It's just wrong. It got all messed up. I mean I am satisfied that I'm out of TCP, but if you look at my schedule, it looks like I'm not motivated or living up to my potential. I mean [taking night courses at a community college] is a possibility, but when? . . . And then, I think, I think I *might* take trig honors next year [which she believed would make her schedule look more rigorous], and I can always write an essay explaining all this to some college . . . but I don't want my senior year to be too intense. So, I don't know. My counselor says just make sure I get A's—which I am basically doing, and I am not in a show right now, but I am still pretty busy with [music and Thespian clubs]. I don't know , I am still sooo con-fu-u-used. . . .

She draws out these last words for emphasis, pats both her cheeks, rolls her eyes, and sighs. She was continually having to make unsatisfactory choices. Last year she considered dropping out of school and believed it might have been the only way to "keep from stressing out." This year, after transferring from TCP to be able to continue to star in drama productions, she worried that her transcript might look "weak" to potential colleges. She was still not sure that she wanted to go to college and had flirted with the idea of "trying to make it as a professional actress" after her senior year, but she didn't want to cut off "any future possibilities." She even took the SATs in March "just in case." She was upset about her combined score of 1200 though and reluctantly planned to take the tests again in June after she had more time to prepare.[5] She disliked spending time studying for an exam that tested "stuff never used in everyday life," but such drudgery had to be done to conform with college expectations.

In fact, Michelle believed that much of what she was learning in school was about conformity and "playing the system":

> What this place has done is like, it's really subtle, I mean there's just the way that they [the school people] go about things—and you know like you get an A by playing the teacher really, 'cause you do what they want and then you're done. . . . It's not hard really. I mean people are so unmotivated, and all you have to do is figure out what the teacher wants, memorize it, and give it back. It's just that other people don't do as well because they don't care. . . . So if you can, if you learn how to manipulate the system, then you learn how you can survive in high school without going nuts.

Michelle compared herself to many of the other students in her classes who were noticeably unmotivated to succeed according to the standards their teachers set. She purposely chose to "play," memorizing material and "giving it back" on tests and assignments as a strategy for manipulating the system. If she "played the teachers" in these easy classes, she believed she could win favors in the form of trust and freedom. She believed that, as in her math class, her high grades and her willingness to please would allow her the flexibility to pursue other interests. At the very least, she believed that the grades and status she achieved would work to her advantage in the event that she decided to go to college. She had yet to find a satisfying way to meet her intellectual needs at the school, though, and was still frustrated that she was required to learn subjects in "bits and pieces." She could not find many peers who shared her excitement for learning or teachers who would encourage her to "let [her] imagination run wild,"[6] but she did eventually manage to set up a schedule that allowed her some measure of freedom. Her easy courses enabled her to pursue her passion for drama and music, and in these performing arts classes Michelle found the excitement, support, and, for the most part, the collegiality that was missing in her other courses.

MICHELLE
SPENCE

Learning by Doing What You Love

Michelle's earliest memory as a child is playing Scrooge in a play at her father's pre-school. She describes the time as "one of the funnest" in her life and recalls some details specifically:

> All the kids got a part . . . and I remember this broken plastic hat that I wore, top hat, black. It was always annoying me. . . . I remember we set up so there would be lights coming on to four different corners of the room—instead of like changing scenes we would just change the focus of the audience. . . . And I remember doing this one part, I was always the one who remembered my lines and everyone else was always late and I'd be sitting there going chee, chee, chee [a stage whisper], you know, the annoying one who's prompting the lines to my friends, but they loved me for it. Yeah, and we'd do all sorts of little shows like that for the parents, and it was always really fun.

Though she did some drama activities in elementary school, she re-discovered her love for acting during her sophomore year when she was cast in a small role in a one-act play. Her success in that role led to a major part in a serious play that showcased her talent as a

leading actress. Since then, Michelle had starred in four productions at the school and established herself as a leader in the
drama department. She helped to form a new Thespian Club
where she was elected "co-president"; she served on the committee
to select students for the advanced acting classes; she worked on
ways to raise money for the drama and music programs, including
procuring funds to replace the dilapidated stage and outdated
equipment in the school cafeteria; and she acted as a de facto teaching assistant to Ms. Fogarty who often relied on her to critique
other drama students and to manage any crises that occurred during class or play rehearsals.

Michelle gladly accepted these leadership responsibilities. She
considered Ms. Fogarty "an excellent teacher and a really great director . . . a mentor" whom she wished to support "in any way possible." She called the teacher by her first name, Lisa, and valued their
close friendship. Michelle spent most of her free periods in Lisa's
office where she (along with a few other students) was given free
access to the computer and printer as well as the comfortable chairs
and work tables. Often, four or five students would crowd into the
office with Lisa and Michelle to share Chinese food and discuss future production plans. Usually Michelle stayed on to chat and to
ask questions about a play she was reading for independent study.
Sometimes Lisa invited Michelle out to lunch or offered to drive
her home from school where the two would brainstorm ideas for
staging scenes in a current production. They worked well together,
at times finishing each other's sentences or predicting what the
other was thinking, and they came to rely upon one another for
support. When Michelle needed guidance during her crisis with
TCP, Lisa served as her main advisor, and when Lisa struggled
with morning sickness from a difficult pregnancy, Michelle "stood

guard" at her office door making sure that nobody disturbed her while she rested during free periods.

The two shared a kind of relationship that was rare in my observations at the school. Usually the hectic pace of the school day and the large number of students in the classes hindered any kind of sustained personal interaction between teacher and student. But Lisa spent long hours with her students in rehearsals and welcomed them into her office throughout the day. Her kindness and generosity made them feel at ease with her, and her excitement about the drama program was contagious. Many students admired her and chose to be involved with the productions, offering to spend extra hours helping to paint sets or sew costumes. In part, the students were drawn to the opportunity to do tasks not usually associated with traditional courses, such as setting up lights and dancing in chorus lines, which had to be done skillfully to meet the expectations of "real" audiences and fellow cast members.[7] The students, however, were also clearly drawn to Ms. Fogarty herself, and the drama program would not have been nearly as appealing without her creative and sensitive leadership. One parent told me that Lisa "changed [her] son's life." Her constant support and enthusiasm helped him to get over his fear of speaking in public and "drew him out of his shell."

Of the students who described themselves as part of the "drama crowd," many considered Michelle to be the "best actress in the school" and knew that she was Lisa's star pupil. In class the teacher would credit Michelle for her helpful ideas by saying for instance, "Michelle and I were just talking, and we thought it would be neat if we moved this group of actors to the front and put the staircase here." She would use Michelle as an example for others to follow: "Listen to how Michelle gets her voice above the choir—that's how

MICHELLE
SPENCE

I want you to project." The other students seemed to accept Michelle's special status and often sought her advice. They asked her to watch them rehearse scenes and practice monologues, and she was happy to help. She confidently gave direction: "Say it like this. . . . That's good; remember you are angry here and are in a power position behind the chair." Before the students took the stage, Michelle offered words of encouragement, "Don't worry. You'll do great."

Michelle felt comfortable playing the role of teacher's assistant in drama, though she notes that this was not always the case in her other classes:

> There's a dangerous line between showing your stuff versus people seeing you as a know-it-all or teachers thinking that you overstep boundaries. You are considered a kiss-up if you really try to learn, like really try to be interactive, because you'd be the only one doing it most likely. Sometimes I want to really show my stuff and sometimes I don't.

Often Michelle would lie about her high grades to students in her math and psychology courses for fear that they would resent her, or worse yet, ask to cheat off her paper during the next exam. This strategy of hiding her motivation to learn or not wanting to reveal her strong skills seems to contrast greatly with Kevin and Eve's strategies for trying to appear knowledgeable and well-prepared in many of their courses. They seemed more concerned with gaining the teachers' approval and less worried about how their peers might react to this behavior, perhaps because they believed their peers were busy playing the same game. "Being interactive" and appearing to really want to learn was valued in their classes by teachers and students alike, more for the potential to raise one's grades, than for the genuine merit of the act.

Fortunately, in Michelle's drama class students were encouraged to work together to help make the production as good as it could be. There was no way to really "cheat" on stage, and rather than judging Michelle as a "kiss-up," the other students appreciated her talent and congratulated her on her fine work. They were all expected to participate fully in the class, and, given the nature of the subject, it was difficult for students to "hide" their success (or lack of preparation) from their peers. During a production, the students literally spent every afternoon and evening together, sometimes working as late as 2 AM, and they grew to consider themselves "as family," often greeting one another with hugs when they passed in the hallways. Like the closeness Michelle felt toward her friends at Horizons Elementary, she enjoyed the support and affection she found with the high school drama crowd; with them, she felt comfortable showing her "real self" and openly working to perfect her craft.

MICHELLE
SPENCE

She also enjoyed the real sense of challenge she experienced when she prepared for and performed a role. Each play offered a different "hurdle" to be overcome and new lessons to be learned. She explains:

> You learn about yourself, you learn about peers, you learn about humanity and all the subjects that the play promotes. . . . Like in the play *For Colored Girls Who Considered Suicide,* that was one of the hardest things I've ever done in my life because, like, everybody that was in that cast was black except for me, and I've never been in a situation where I was that much of a minority before, and it's like culture shock. . . . And you know I was going to quit because I felt so isolated, but I stayed with it. And you know I was overwhelmed by the way, their, they seemed to be so talented and do everything so naturally. But I worked my butt off for that part, and I mean what I accomplished was really

MICHELLE
SPENCE amazing I feel. I mean I'm proud of what I did. Even if it wasn't the best that I could have done, that's what I did, and um and so when it was all over with I had, not only had I like reached another level with acting, but also I dropped a lot of racism that I didn't even know I had which was just from being in the society.

Performing in this play allowed Michelle to grow in ways she had not experienced in her other classes. Initially, she felt "overwhelmed"—as she was not sure she could meet the challenges presented to her.[8] But, after much hard work, she was able to feel proud of what she achieved and reflect on the experience as one of great learning. She felt genuinely changed by the play—as if she had "broken down some major walls" in herself; she had not considered herself "racist" before, but she soon realized that many of her reactions stemmed from unfair beliefs she held about others. The play helped her to identify more closely with the lives of African Americans and with oppressed people in general and caused her to reexamine some deeply held beliefs about herself and humanity.[9]

Michelle performed in four other plays that year, all of which challenged her in particular ways and served as sources of engagement. Her role of the grandmother in the musical *Pippin* for instance "terrified" her at first. She had never sung in front of a live audience before (she had just recently joined the music groups at school), and the role demanded that she sing several solo parts. She describes the experience as one of great risk-taking:

It's been a lot of work. I had to be independent with my character. At first I was conservative, like a regular grandma, and Lisa said, "Give it more." I didn't want to take risks but I did. It's the challenge that pushes you to achieve the best you can. I am completely exhausted and really behind in all my classes. Sometimes rehearsals go to 3 in the morning, and then on the night of the

play we have to strike [the set] for people to use the cafeteria. . . . But it is worth it. When you work in a show you have
energy from cast and audience, and you run off this energy,
and they feed off yours, and you have closeness like a family. . . .
I was so scared but I did it anyway, and when I do that, it just, I
think that was one of the best performances you know that I've
ever done. It's the thing that I'm most proud of the whole year.

MICHELLE
SPENCE

Michelle's hard work with this role was evident and the results
were impressive. I had never seen her so immersed in a part and so
alive on stage. The play had been a bit tedious until her main scene;
the acting and staging were fine, but the actors lacked a sense of
timing and showed little excitement in their performances. When
Michelle stepped on stage, the audience was transformed. Dressed
in a faded yellow daisy dress with lace trim, gray powdered hair in
a bun, stockings rolled down her skinny legs in clumps around the
ankles, spectacles at the tip of her nose, and sporting a long gray
cane that she shook vigorously at the other characters when she
spoke, Michelle was no longer herself. Suddenly we were in the
presence of a scowling and mettlesome 80-year-old grandmother
who sang in a crackly doddering voice a spirited rendition of
"Whole Lot of Livin'," shaking her rear end and shimmying her
shoulders to prove that though she was old, she still had plenty of
life left in her. The song inspired a standing ovation from the crowd
and injected a much-needed boost of energy into the rest of the
play. I overheard one teacher later that week commenting on
Michelle's star performance:

I saw her play the old lady, and I was *sure* it was a professional. I
said to myself, no teenager could do a job that well. Did you see
how she made her mouth go down in a scowl like that? She was
great.

MICHELLE
SPENCE

Michelle explains that she thrives on the challenges the roles present her, and like Teresa, who seeks opportunities for "pushing herself," Michelle equates learning and growth with taking risks and venturing outside her comfort zones. When the risks are genuine, when they have real consequences, Michelle is inspired to face her fears and work harder on her performances. She talks about wanting to "live up to [her] potential" as an actress and admits that she is a "perfectionist" who wants to act on a level "better than that of a high school performer." Even when her peers and Lisa award her perfect scores on her monologues and scenes in class, Michelle is not pleased until she believes she has done "the best that [she] can do." Because of this, she craves constructive criticism as a way of pushing herself to excel:

> Lisa allows you to create your art, and she doesn't always push you. But I need criticism. Someone needs to criticize me so I can know I am doing good. . . . One of the things is when people say like, "Oh you're so good, you're you're . . . you know, one of the best actresses I know," that's not much of a compliment I don't feel because it's hard to know if they're telling the truth or if they're just buttering you over, so I never trust that, and then there's not much competition at our school. I mean like the level I don't feel is yet to be impressive in acting. My dad will tell the truth though, I mean he will tell me the truth. He'll tell me because he knows that's what I need. That's what I want, and I won't accept anything else otherwise I won't trust him. So he tells me the bad things. I've trained him that way. . . . And now I ask Lisa to be really honest with me.

When the audience leaps to their feet, when her father gives praise, when the drama professors serving as judges at the drama competition award her first place out of 100 other actors, when an agent recruits her for a local theater company, Michelle feels proud of her accomplishments. These are sources of real criticism for her, and they help her to know when she has successfully met the challenge of the role. Because she is one of the best actresses in the school, traditional forms of assessment such as comments and grades from her teacher and peers are not enough to convince her of her merits.

MICHELLE
SPENCE

Understanding Michelle's desire for learning and growth, Lisa cast her in one of the most difficult roles of the year, that of the stage manager in the play *Our Town*. At first, Michelle complained about the part. There were "too many lines to memorize" and no "real character to develop." She worried that the audience would be bored and that she wouldn't be able to "pull it off":

> I can't do it. I have no clue. I mean it's a real stretch for me, which is good, I guess. I mean that's what the class is for, right? . . . But I'm just not sure how to play it, like how is the audience going to respond to all this talking?

A few days before the show, Michelle was still struggling with the role. She said her lines quickly, not knowing which parts to emphasize, and she continued to worry. She said, "I really don't like this part. I am still so, so lost." She was upset that Lisa had been too busy to work closely with her and help her to develop the part, and she was frustrated that she had not been able to do it on her own.

During an evening performance of the play, I watched Michelle competently deliver her monologues and perform the duties of the stage manager, but I observed that she lacked the verve and connection with the audience noticeable in her other performances. Afterward, many people congratulated her and told her she was "terrific," but she brushed off the compliments. The following week she reflected on the experience and what made it so difficult for her:

MICHELLE
SPENCE

It was my worst role all year, and I was never happy with the part. Even my dad agrees it is my worst performance. And on the last night I had like a nervous breakdown. . . . I broke down completely; I was, like, bawling my eyes out before the play because I was so unhappy with what I had done with myself, with my performance. It was just such a horrible feeling, I mean I was going through it and I couldn't get it right, just I, it sounded horrible and fake, just memorized and everything was going wrong with it, and I just started to collapse. . . . Even when Lisa was saying "good job" because I see her say "good job" to people who I believe have real problems, and I think how do I trust that she's not leaving stuff out for me? I mean she's in a public high school, and if there's a kid up there doing their best and it's horrible, she can't say "bad job" because then it might totally destroy their whole self-opinion. . . .

And what happened was she sat me down and she was like, "OK," and she gave me a talk about how what I was doing was I was forgetting that a play isn't a play. You're supposed to have fun, and you're supposed to *play* with it. . . . And the thing, probably the reason that this wasn't my best performance was that I just came to a point where all I was doing was beating myself up and I wouldn't let go. I mean I cared so much about how I was looking and what I was doing that it was too coarse. So I guess it just showed me what happens when I get too overdone with not allowing myself to achieve what I want.

Just as Eve strives for perfection in her classes, Michelle sets high standards for herself in drama. She takes her work very seriously especially because it is the only class where she feels engaged with the material. When she is unable to develop the stage manager role to her satisfaction, she "breaks down" and needs to be convinced to

"play," to have fun. She has become so used to succeeding in
school that she does not know how to face the possibility of "fail- MICHELLE
ing," at least in her eyes. At Horizons Elementary, Michelle felt SPENCE
free to make mistakes and to learn from the process while having
fun, but at Faircrest it was rare for her to feel genuinely challenged,
let alone comfortable with the notion that she might not reach her
standards for perfection each time. In drama class Michelle was encouraged to try new roles and to explore material that interested
her, but even with this freedom, she had lost some sense of "play."
Our Town provided a good lesson—that it was important to
struggle toward a goal but that it was as important not to berate
oneself when the goal seemed out of reach. She believed that surely
there would be other challenges that might elude her, and that she
needed to face these as opportunities for learning instead of moments for despair.

At the end of the semester Michelle still worried that her transfer out of TCP into the easy classes had somehow tainted her future
possibilities for college, but she reiterated her conviction that she
had made the right choice and believed that the experience helped
her "set priorities":

> I was really sick of this school because of all the pressure, and I
> mean you get a couple letters home saying "Oh congratulations,
> you're a 4.0 student blah, blah, blah. . . ." And then that just got
> me stuck on the whole achieving process . . . 'cause it led me to
> feel like in some odd way that if I didn't succeed then I wouldn't
> be remembered, or I'd be caught up in like a little office job
> doing something I hated. . . . But I'm proud that I left [TCP]. . . .
> Academically I stepped back but I had to leave when I did, and
> leaving made me stronger. . . . I just know that I'm not going to
> let myself get stuck doing something that I don't enjoy doing.

MICHELLE
SPENCE

Like the other students in this study, Michelle sees a connection between what she learns in high school and her future career, and she worries that she won't "succeed" in life if she doesn't succeed academically. She also realizes the absurdity of a system that places so much emphasis on grades and shows so little concern for an individual's academic needs. She understands the value of enjoying the process of learning and of finding the freedom to pursue her own academic interests. In one sense, Michelle discovers this kind of freedom and support in the drama department under the guidance of a caring teacher and among supportive peers, but she is frustrated with the sacrifices she is forced to make to continue doing something she loves. She believes she "played the system well" in order to "survive without going nuts," but she wonders what high school might have been like had it been organized around the same principles as Horizons Elementary. Had some of her classes been organized to better meet her needs, to teach subjects more cohesively, to provide students more opportunities for following their curiosity, and to promote cooperative learning instead of fostering competition, Michelle believes she might have felt more satisfied with her high school experience.

CHAPTER 6

Roberto Morales:
When Values Stand in the Way

When Roberto was in the fourth grade, his aunt used to drive to his house each evening to help him with his reading. He had trouble understanding many of the English vocabulary words and was falling behind his classmates. He knew his aunt was tired after a long day at work, but she "was always there for [him], no matter what," helping him to make sense of the stories and answer the study questions. As he describes the many hours she and other family members spent with him, Roberto wipes tears from his eyes. He is grateful for the support of his family and feels "blessed by the spirit they give [him] to believe in [himself]."

> My family, they're like behind me 100 percent. Whatever I do, they're there for me all the time, you know. They go, "If you need help in anything, call me up any time of hour. . . ." And they're really fascinated that I, you know, so early in my age . . . already decided I want to go to college and want to major in [electrical

ROBERTO
MORALES

engineering], and, you know, I announced that during Christmas in front of everybody. That was like a Christmas gift I give
to everybody, and my mom and my grandma were crying, they
were all happy and all "Oh you're going to go on and go to college," and everything like that. Like 'cause, um, like in my family . . . only two out of so many family members have gone [to
college] and having another family member going to college is
like a big thing. . . . My mom didn't go to college and my dad
didn't either, and you know, I want to show an example to my
sister 'cause she looks up to me. . . . You know, seeing people are
right there behind me puts my spirits up, makes me want to
shoot for it no matter what.

Roberto's family moved to the suburbs several years ago, about an
hour's drive from his aunt and uncle's apartment, but he still receives
help with his homework when he visits on weekends. His mother,
too, offers help when she gets home from work at a local store, especially with some of the assignments from his Spanish class. And
though his stepfather's job as a truck driver keeps him away from
home for several weeks at a time, Roberto and he managed to work
together on a report for English class about their family's Latin
American roots. Roberto refers to this report as one of the most
important school projects of the year because, he says, it brought
him closer to his dad and allowed the two of them to see each other
"for more than just at the dinner table every now and then."[1]

Roberto's family and close friends call him Berto or Bertito and
affectionately describe him as "a genius." He tells a story of bringing
some homework down to the pool after an afternoon of swimming
with friends in his apartment complex. When a few of the neighborhood boys saw his textbooks, they commented on his dedication to school and the impressive course load he was carrying:

My friends were all, "Whoa, you're in advanced algebra?" . . . "Man, you're so smart, you're like a genius, you should like tutor me." And I do tutor some of them, and my mom was out there and my dad and they were all like proud of their son and everything, doing their little smile and everything. And I was thinking, they're exaggerating too much, you know.

ROBERTO
MORALES

His cousin, who is a year older and also attends Faircrest, agrees with the friends: "It's embarrassing how much smarter he is than me, and he's only a tenth grader! . . . That's my cousin, the A student!" Berto blushes and tries to play down the compliment: "She helps me with English and I help her with math; we swap." Another friend joins in, "He has so many credits, man, he could practically graduate this year!"

Later, Roberto explains that many of his neighborhood friends don't do well in school. He is one of the few in the group who takes college preparatory courses and studies hard, and he is the only one who consistently gets A's and B's on his report card. He is frustrated by his friends' lack of motivation and is upset that his attempts to help them have been ignored:

Some of them, they just, like, they really don't care. And, like, I get mad at them. I just, like, I sock 'em. I just hit 'em. . . . I just go BAM [pretending to sock my arm], "What the hell is wrong with you? You need help, why don't you just come to me?" Sometimes they do, I'm surprised [when] they do, but most, it's like they really don't care. Like the guy who just came up to me, you know. I think he, he says he failed English and he failed world studies, and I think he failed math. It's like, it's like, "I told you come to me." He goes . . . "No, just leave me alone, leave me alone."

ROBERTO
MORALES

This display of anger is unusual for Berto. He is worried about these friends because he has seen older boys in the apartment complex whose school apathy has led them to "ruin their lives with drugs or gangs." Berto is resolved not to be one of them and wishes he could convince his friends to "believe in themselves and care about school" as he does.[2]

Because Berto is in separate classes from these boys, and because he spends much of his free time studying, he rarely interacts with his neighborhood friends during school hours. Instead, he prefers to hang out with classmates, whom he describes as his "smart, white friends." Together, they walk the hallways of the school, singing silly songs and cracking jokes. In PE class, they chat incessantly and try to whine their way out of the required warm-up exercises. They unsuccessfully attempt to boycott a mandatory mile run around the outdoor track in 90 degree weather. When the teacher insists on the exercise, they opt to jog backwards "in protest," with Berto leading the way in a crazy prance that makes the others laugh. In other classes, such as biology, algebra, and English, Berto and these friends are mostly serious and attentive, sometimes passing notes to one another, but usually quiet, polite, and focused on the task at hand.

In fact, Berto is one of the few students I observe who regularly listens to and follows his teachers' instructions. When they ask for quiet, Berto closes his mouth. When they say, "get busy," Berto opens his book and begins to work on the assignment. He consistently treats the teachers with respect, and because of this good behavior, most of his teachers seem to trust him and treat him well in return. Many ask him to do small favors like running a message to the attendance office or helping to decorate a bulletin board. One teacher even asked Berto if he would mind sharing his locker with a new transfer student for a few weeks until she received her own. Usually Berto acquiesces to each request, even when some tasks

cause him inconvenience, such as being late to class. His positive
attitude and smiling face endear him to others, especially several
female students who develop crushes on him and slip love notes
into his textbooks, occasionally tickling the back of his neck when
they are fortunate enough to grab the seat immediately behind him.

ROBERTO
MORALES

At work, too, Berto is well-liked and sought-after. He works as
an assistant manager at a local fast food restaurant approximately
20 to 30 hours per week. He is supposed to work seven hours a day
on weekends and Friday afternoons, but lately he has been assigned
the 4 to 10 PM shift on many weekdays as well. He admits that all
these hours at the restaurant are interfering with his school work,
but he is being trained to be a manager, and "even though there are
laws about how many hours you can work [as a minor], the em-
ployers always need you." They count on Roberto to help write the
daily reports, make the time sheets, and do computer work, especially because many of the full-time managers don't speak English
well and aren't skilled with computers. Berto is proud of his work,
explaining that he is "a leader" there and that "it is exciting to learn
real life skills like how to treat people and how to handle problems."
Still, he wishes he could find a "better balance between work and
school." He needs the money to pay for school supplies, clothes,
lunches, transportation, "almost everything," because his parents
have little money to share. In fact, Berto's stepfather owes him $800.
Berto hopes that things will improve when he passes his driver's test
this summer; then he can drive to work and save the lengthy travel
time by bus from school to the restaurant, or, better yet, he can get
a higher paying job at the supermarket once he turns sixteen.

Hailed as a genius by family and friends, well-liked and trusted
by many of his teachers, and respected by his co-workers, Berto, by
all accounts, should feel happy with himself and his achievements.
But he is plagued by anxiety about his future. Will he be able to get

into the college of his choice? Will he be able to fulfill his dream of becoming an electrical engineer? Will he be able to "keep up the high grades," as his school counselor advised him? How will he balance work, school, and family commitments? And, he wonders, as much as he studies, why isn't he able to get the A grades his "smart" friends receive—especially when he seems to be working as hard as his peers?

Though his parents and teachers are pleased with his 3.4 GPA last semester, Berto is not content:

> I'm shooting for A's in all my classes, but I don't know. I put myself down too much. . . . Too much low esteem, but it's hard, I mean, I give myself all I got and I don't get what I want. Like, I give all my studying habits everything I got. I study every hour every time—I, I even leave the house when there's too much noise or I kick everybody out of the house. I tell them, "Go, here's some money, go eat or something." I study, I tell them, "Don't come back 'til I call you or something." And when it comes to the point of the test, I blank out, and that really annoys me, and then when I find out the grade, that annoys me the most. . . .

> I just wish I could get a 4.0. I just want to feel the excitement of getting it, I want to *feel* it—a 4.0. My friend got one last semester and he's like a regular person. He puts his problems aside and does his work. I could do that. I *want* to do that.

Like Kevin and Eve and countless others, Berto is a victim of the grade trap. His school experience has become a quest for a high GPA, not because it represents a body of knowledge learned well, but because of what the school, teachers, counselors, community, colleges, and others have caused the GPA to become. For Berto, a 4.0 represents much more than the possibility of getting into Berke-

ley (his first choice college) or pleasing his family or even succeeding in school; for him, a 4.0 means, "going to that extra level," **ROBERTO**
measuring up to his "smart friends," and being able to believe **MORALES**
that he is "intelligent . . . not just smart enough to pass your classes,
intelligent smart."

This year, at least, such a goal eludes Berto. Despite his hard work
and laudable achievements, Berto feels he has "let [himself] down"
by not achieving a 4.0. Successful in the eyes of others, Berto will
not be pleased until he achieves what some of his friends have, and
though his quest for a perfect GPA proves to be a valuable source
of motivation for him, it also becomes a great source of frustration:
Why doesn't his work ethic pay off?

Diligence

Roberto's modus operandi in school is to "sit down, do the work,
and get it out of the way." He liked to go straight home after classes
on the days he was not required to be at the restaurant and spend
two to three hours doing homework. He carefully entered his assignments into a little datebook the size of his palm and checked
each off accordingly when it was completed. Sometimes though, on
work nights, he didn't get home until 10 or 11 PM and worried that
he was falling behind schedule. On these evenings, he would only
have time to do the homework assignments for one or two classes
and would have to rush to finish the rest during break and lunch
hours. Though this hectic pace was commonplace for students like
Kevin and Eve, Berto wasn't used to the frantic last minute dash to
get papers and problem sets in on time. He would become quiet
and sullen and upset with himself for not staying up later or wak-
ing up earlier to do the work. After a particularly stressful morning, Berto explains:

ROBERTO
MORALES

I just don't like to leave things 'til the last minute. I used to do that last year . . . but still [got things] in on time. I don't like to do that anymore. I should not work on weekdays because it is too big a stress to wait 'til the last minute. We've been studying stress in health class and I don't need it.

During his classes, Berto tried to be just as diligent. When the teachers offered students time in the period to begin their homework or to read ahead, Berto was one of the few who opened his books immediately and got to work. Though he occasionally chatted with friends or was sidetracked reading love notes, Berto usually paid close attention to the teachers and took careful notes. When more than half the class might be goofing off or daydreaming, Berto could be found with his eyes on the board or his head in a book. And unlike many of the students in this study who were in the habit of doing multiple tasks while they were supposed to be listening to a lecture or working on homework problems, Berto rarely used class time to do work in other subjects. Instead, he liked to finish assignments ahead of time and offer help to others. For example, in Spanish class, he managed to complete the vocabulary exercises before anyone else, and, unsolicited, he approached a student waiting for the teacher's attention and offered to help her with the words she didn't understand. Similarly, in biology, he completed the lab and graph work before most of the other students who had spent 20 minutes discussing television shows. One boy noticed Roberto's multicolored graph and yelled, "Berto's done? He must have cheated." Roberto replied, "Berto doesn't cheat." This was true; instead, he used his time wisely.

Another strategy Roberto employed was to try to read books, especially novels assigned in English class, more than once. With a dictionary by his side, Berto struggled to read each book the first time "just for understanding the words and the story." Then, he would strive to read the entire book again with an eye for detail and "deeper meaning." This semester, he managed to read both *I Know Why the Caged Bird Sings* and *Bless Me Ultima* in this manner—an impressive feat, given how little extra time he had for schoolwork. Still, he was frustrated that he wasn't able to read other assigned books more than once and believed his test scores suffered because of this.

ROBERTO MORALES

Aware of the strategies he used to get ahead, Roberto characterizes himself as a hard worker: "I'm working always my hardest, always, all the time. There's no time that I can lag off." He is also quick to admit that he owes part of his success to his ability to get help when needed:

> I'm not saying I'm the smart guy, you know, I get 100 percent sometimes, and it doesn't mean 'cause I'm a nerd or I cram quick. It's 'cause I get help and it, it's not, I shouldn't be ashamed to get help. There's nothing to be ashamed of. . . . Last year I got C's in English mostly because I am a bad writer, but I didn't get any help. I was ashamed and embarrassed to say I needed it. I didn't know anyone to ask. This year I know lots of people to ask, and I'm not embarrassed because even smart people need help sometimes.

Berto often spent his lunch hour in the school's peer tutorial center where he sought help specifically on English and math assignments.[3] He says his peers usually explain concepts more clearly than the textbook or teacher:

> In English, you know, I read all the time. I never lag off on my reading, and there's some things that I don't understand. I ask for help with the teachers but still I get confused. And then when

ROBERTO
MORALES
I ask one of my friends, you know, I understand better. So, it's, it feels better when I ask somebody my own age; I understand what they're talking about. . . . They use simple terms, simple English.

Berto credits a course called Seminar on Studying (S.O.S.) for helping him to understand the advantages of getting help from one's teachers and peers. According to the Faircrest course guide, the S.O.S. course is a "support class for students underrepresented in higher education. . . . The course helps prepare students for college entrance examinations and promotes individual responsibility for college preparation and continual learning" (p. 5). Enrollment is limited mostly to students of color or non-native English speakers who maintain a 2.5 GPA or higher and who show a desire to go to college. Students are encouraged to take the course all four years of high school as it offers practice in writing, note-taking, reading, research, and public speaking skills, as well as tutorial support twice a week where students are free to ask for help on homework assignments. The course also includes opportunities for students to visit local colleges and to participate in community service by working with elementary school students from impoverished neighborhoods.

Berto used the in-class tutorial time effectively each week, asking some of the older students for help with difficult math problems, reading silently at his desk, or speaking to the S.O.S. teacher, Ms. Evans, about his low grades in English. The teacher helped Berto develop a plan for improving his writing skills and offered to go over some notes with him on *All Quiet on the Western Front* to prepare for next week's test. As she did with the other students in the class, Ms. Evans showed a keen interest in Berto's success and spent considerable time working with him to hone his study skills.

She knew that he needed practice speaking in public and often asked him to repeat his comments in class, "This time more loudly, using good eye contact, slo-ow-ly please." Berto took no offense at her comments; he appreciated her help and said that one of the "best parts of the semester was that Ms. Evans was always there for me" helping with homework, helping with leadership and speaking skills, and "calming me down." Here Berto refers to the time when he had an argument with a relative in the school parking lot. He was extremely upset and "ready to fight" when he passed Ms. Evan's classroom after school:

ROBERTO MORALES

> She asked me what was wrong, you know. I didn't tell her what happened, but she knew I was like mad or stuff, and she, you know, just calmed me down. She say, "Relax, relax," and she kept me there throughout . . . until I was calm, but I never told her what happened.

Like Teresa and Michelle, Berto had found an advocate at the school, someone he could rely upon for help, who was willing to listen and who understood his needs.

Recognizing the importance of getting help from others, Berto spent considerable time giving help of his own. He regularly tutored two students in the peer tutorial center, even when he was worried about finishing his own work for the week. He explains that by teaching others, he learns the concepts better himself and, besides, he enjoys doing the service.

> It's great to help people. . . . You know, I been tutoring a girl for geometry also, and I'm going slow, a slow pace so she's understanding, you know. She got a, she got a B on her quiz so she thanked me. And basically when I see the text, I read it and she doesn't understand it. I put [it] in simpler terms, I mean that

ROBERTO
MORALES

she really would understand, and it kicks in. . . . They understand what I'm saying, and it feels good to help somebody 'cause you can make a big difference in their grade.

He also tutors an elementary student each week through his S.O.S. course: When Berto arrives at the classroom, his young "buddy" jumps into his arms and talks excitedly about his day. Berto carries the boy over to his desk and offers encouragement as the youngster revises and illustrates a story, advising him to "fill the page with color" and to "be nice" and share his crayons with a neighbor. They end each session by reading a storybook: "Usually I make him read to me for good practice. I want to show him that reading is fun since no one ever showed me that." Berto looked forward to each of these tutoring sessions. They represented a time when he could stop thinking about his own grades and could feel good about what he was helping others to accomplish.

In Spanish class, too, Berto played the role of an unofficial teaching assistant, helping to translate words and check students' work. Sometimes he had four or five students clamoring around his desk, preventing him from completing his own assignments. When he had been interrupted several times one morning by students seeking help, he playfully announced, "Berto is dead right now, but if you please leave your name and number." Moments later he turned to the students and said, "No, just kidding, what did you ask?" The teacher appreciated Berto's help but wrongly assumed that the class was easy for him. The teacher explains, "Berto doesn't work hard, but he has a natural intelligence. He should probably be in honors Spanish, but many native speakers don't go into honors [courses] because they don't want the extra work." Berto studied hard for Spanish, as he did for his other courses; his abundant Spanish vocabulary combined with his willingness to help gave the appearance of being overqualified for the course. When the teacher saw Berto's low B grades on tests, he assumed Berto was lazy and lacked interest. My observations indicated that Berto received the less-than-perfect scores because he had difficulty with verb conjugations and because he suffered extreme anxiety when taking tests and speaking in public, anxiety that affected his grades in almost every course, not just Spanish.

ROBERTO
MORALES

Anxiety

Thursday, February 7, 8:10 AM: I watch as Berto moans his way through an English test on *All Quiet on the Western Front*. I know that he has read the entire book and that he "really liked it," especially the action sequences. I know that he studied for the test last night and that Ms. Evans helped him to understand the class notes on the book. And yet, my stomach sinks when I see his expression as the teacher passes out the exam. He points to the quotation identification section and asks nervously, "What happens if we miss a few of these?" The teacher just smiles and continues to distribute the test. Five minutes later, Berto rubs his neck and says sadly to himself, "I don't know." He puts his head down on the desk and rests briefly, staring into space. Frowning, he picks up the pencil and tries to formulate answers to the detailed questions. He scribbles and stops, scribbles and stops. Fifteen minutes pass, and before any of the other students begin working on the second page, Berto walks up and hands in the exam. He looks miserable as he takes his seat again and reluctantly opens his book to check his answers. "Damn!" he says in a whisper. "I failed." A few minutes later, a couple students turn in their exams. Berto closes his book and sighs, "I don't care."

Over and over, as I saw with Teresa, Berto struggled through exams. He studied hard, often proving that he knew the material

ROBERTO
MORALES

well in the review session the day before, answering the biology or math questions out loud before most of the other students had a chance to look up the information. Then, on the day of the test, he would "go blank."

> I get nervous and paralyzed, and I got this from my mom because she had like the same problem in high school. I start looking at it and say, "What is this?"

> I understand it as much as everybody understands it, but the point, the thing is, is why, why did I get a B, you know, and this person got an A if we both know the same material and it's my fault that, that I could blank out on a test and do so poorly? . . . When it comes to the test, it's like oh my God I just don't, you know, I just forget. And then they come out with an A and I come out with a B, and I'd like, it just like puts me down more. . . because it puts my self esteem down even though I try to prove to everybody I could accomplish getting a 4.0. . . . It's too hard 'cause all the pressure. . . . Maybe teachers shouldn't base everything on grades . . . because people learn in their own ways.

Berto emphasized this point several times during the semester. He believed he studied as hard as his friends, sometimes studying with them, seeming to know the information equally well. But he could not achieve the grades they did. He blamed his "test-anxiety" on heredity (he says he "inherited a bad memory") and on the extreme pressure he felt from his family and peers to do well. Though his family and friends and S.O.S. classmates were his greatest source of support, they also contributed to his ongoing sense of pressure. He didn't want to let them down. He wanted to go to Berkeley like his uncle and become an electrical engineer. He regarded every test and every quiz as important steps toward his future goals. As long as his teachers continued to use exams as primary forms of assessment, Berto feared he would never achieve the grades he desired.

His public speaking anxiety stemmed from a different fear: "I hate performing or getting up in front of the class because sometimes I stutter and stuff or mess up, and people laugh." Unlike Teresa, Berto was not as concerned about his accent (which was minimal), but worried more that he would "make a fool of [himself]" and appear unprepared in front of people he "barely knew." Though he seemed confident answering questions from his seat or explaining concepts to others, he was terrified to speak in front of large groups. In health class, Berto was asked to present his Lifestyle Choices Poster to the class. He had created a collage of magazine pictures that made little sense to the audience without some explanation. Though he spent considerable time describing the images on the poster to me earlier that day, when it came time to speak to the class, he panicked. At first he pretended that he couldn't find the poster on the large classroom wall; then, when the teacher located it in the corner of the room, Berto spoke two sentences and sat down. He was frustrated that the teacher gave him such low marks on the presentation and hoped that his S.O.S. class and Ms. Evans' coaching would help him eventually overcome his fear of public speaking.

As frightened as he was to speak in front of the classroom, Berto always managed to get up and say something rather than receive an F grade on the assignment. He didn't understand why some of the students in his Spanish class seemed not to care about their grades and that they opted for F's instead of attempting the oral exercises. He said to his friend, "Don't you care, man? An F!" It bewildered him when students seemed not to play by the rules, not to try for good grades, nor to respect their teachers. Berto believed in following instructions, in giving help to his peers, loaning class notes,

listening to his elders. In spite of his anxiety, he attempted to fulfill his teachers' expectations. He didn't have a sense of how to
do school any other way.

Playing By the Rules

With the possible exception of PE class, where it was a bit of a game
to try to get out of doing warm-up or cool-down exercises, in all his
other classes, Berto labored to "do things right," act respectfully,
and do the assignments correctly. Ironically, at times, his good in-
tentions actually prevented him from accomplishing his goals. For
instance, when Roberto had a question for the teacher, he raised his
hand in accordance with what he believed was considered proper
classroom behavior. When the teacher failed to recognize him, he
continued to raise his hand until he could no longer keep it in the
air. After a few more tries without success, Berto gave up, explaining later that he had forgotten what it was he was going to ask.
When I note that some of the other students simply resort to yelling
out their questions, he shakes his head and says, "Yeah, but that's
just plain rude."

He offers a similar reply when asked why he doesn't interrupt a
teachers' meeting to find out if he qualified for next year's honors-
level math class. Berto had taken the qualifying exam in March and
needed to hear the results at that time in order to determine his
schedule for the following year. He reasoned that he would take
only one honors course next year because he didn't want to overload himself, and he preferred to take honors math because of his
interest in engineering. His friend urged him to walk in and interrupt the meeting to discover his score, "C'mon, Berto, that's what
they are there for!" Berto refused: "No, I can't interrupt. It's *rude!* I
will check later." Unfortunately, Berto hears too late that he did not
pass the exam. He was frustrated because he would not have had to

take the qualifying exam to get into honors math if he'd received
an A in this year's math class (he got an A−). With his test anxiety, he was not surprised by the results, but by the time he heard,
it was too late to get accepted to the honors Spanish class. Another
student might have petitioned the results, argued his way into one
of the honors courses, or had a parent or teacher help him through,
but not Berto. It never crossed his mind to question the qualifying
process nor to reveal the results to Ms. Evans, who might have been
able to intervene on his behalf.

ROBERTO
MORALES

Such mishaps occurred with surprising frequency as Berto
earnestly attempted to follow the rules. For example, in an English
class assignment on *Bless Me Ultima,* the teacher had students
brainstorm a list of important life events and plot three or four of
them on a timeline. Berto quickly jotted twenty listings and, using
a textbook edge to draw a straight line, began to plot four in order.
Minutes later, when most of the students had yet to begin the assignment, the teacher changed her mind: "Why don't you pick out
all the events that you believe are important and list each of these on
your timelines." Upon hearing the new instructions, Berto sighed,
"Ah, man, I messed up." He ripped his paper in half and started the
timeline again. Five minutes later, the teacher altered the directions
a second time, asking students to "leave enough room between
events to write some comments." For many of the students who
were still completing their lists, these directions did not pose a problem, but for Berto, who was used to starting his work once it was assigned, the teacher's changes were frustrating. As he searched for a
bottle of liquid paper to make the requested revisions, he groaned,
"Ah, man!" and shook his head. A different student might have complained to the teacher or, perhaps, might have turned in the flawed
assignment, too frustrated to begin again. Berto persevered, grum-
bling under his breath but never loud enough for the teacher to hear.

ROBERTO
MORALES

Another time, in his pursuit to "do things right," Berto asked so many logistical questions about an assignment, that the teacher and students became frustrated with him. In biology, Berto spent several minutes trying to clarify the teacher's instructions for collecting a lab specimen. He raised his hand and asked about specifics the teacher had not included in the introduction to the assignment: "How much agar should we use exactly? Why put it in all four corners [of the slide]? Where do we put the algae specimen once the steam escapes?" After answering several questions in a row, the teacher grew impatient and said bruskly, "Put it on any flat surface; it just doesn't matter, Roberto!" A few students chimed in, "Yeah, let's get going already." Later, Berto explains to me that he asked so many questions because he knew from experience that it was nearly impossible to get the teacher's attention once the lab was underway. Unlike other students who simply screamed out the teacher's name until they were acknowledged, or busied themselves with computer games until the teacher made his rounds, Berto did not want to act rudely or waste precious time. He understood that he needed to get all the help he could ahead of time, before the lab commenced, if he was to be able to complete the lab requirements correctly and in a timely manner. Unfortunately, the class was not set up to accommodate this kind of strategy. Even though Berto's questions seemed to apply to everyone, the teacher and other students were not used to working this way. They knew they had a limited amount of time to get the work done, and they viewed Berto's inquiries as impositions.

In this case and in the example from the English class above, Berto's values of diligence and politeness actually impede his efforts to do well. He begins his assignments immediately and earnestly, and, in doing so, he differs from the majority of students who lag and fail to listen to directions, or others who show little concern over detailed instructions in class since they know only the final lab report or chapter test will count for a grade. If they miss something, they can always ask a friend or the teacher for help later, in time to complete the final product. Or, they can argue that the teacher's lack of clarity should be taken into account when assessing their grades.

ROBERTO
MORALES

Often when a student like Berto does not act in accordance with the majority of students, teachers are caught off guard. They usually don't have the time to cater to an individual student's needs, and they have come to expect and perhaps rely on the more typical, less diligent, behavior. If Berto, as he believes, studies as hard as his "smart" friends, he may not achieve their high grades, in part, because he does not completely understand the system in which he is acting. Schools are set up, with their tight time schedules and overcrowded classrooms, to demand certain behaviors from students, and Berto has not yet figured out how to behave in a way that meets his own standards for excellence as well as those of the teachers.

Outside of school, too, Roberto struggles to abide by his system of values amidst tensions to do otherwise. At work he believes that people take advantage of him because they know he is a "nice guy." When no one else will work the late shift, the managers call on Berto. He says that he tries to get out of it but that his boss won't let him. He even missed his younger sister's birthday party, an event that was important to him, because he could not get out of work. He knows that other people lie and say that they have "emergencies" or they call in sick, but he doesn't like to do this. "You shouldn't lie," he says seriously, "besides, who else are they gonna get?" Berto hopes he will eventually be rewarded for his dedication to work when he is appointed full manager, but he is frustrated that his honesty and strong work ethic make him easily exploitable. He continues to be disappointed when he tries to play by the rules but does not obtain the results he desires.

Perhaps a more significant example of his vulnerability is when Roberto is accused of cheating during his final project in drawing class fall semester. As he mentions earlier, Berto, as a rule, does not cheat. He believes it is "sinful" and that "God is always watching over your shoulder, so no matter what, you get punished." He admits that cheating is rampant at the high school, but that he has never given in to the temptation:

> Cheating, cheating, it occurs every time, every test, it doesn't matter. . . . Lots of students cheat here. They tend to cheat off kids who are afraid to say no—they threaten to beat them up. . . . They'll look over your shoulder, and you could get in trouble also for . . . them cheating even if you don't know that they're copying off of you. . . . And when you get graded on a curve here, you would lower your grade down to get their grade higher, and that's not fair to the people who really work their butt off to get that high grade.

> For someone who has never cheated in his life, I guess I am surprised that I am doing so well. Cheating just doesn't feel like you accomplish anything, you don't learn the skills for the future, and it's just not worth it. . . . Sometimes I'm tempted because I'm like, "oh my God I don't understand this," but I can't do it. To tell you the truth I get too nervous and I just don't want to do it. I can't look over somebody's shoulder, . . . not even a glance. If I don't understand it, I'll leave it, do the rest of it and go back to it, you know.

In all my observations, I never saw Roberto cheat. I didn't even see him employ some of the subtler, "creative" cheating strategies that some of the others in this study used, such as copying homework or problem sets, missing school on the day of a test to take more time to study, or gathering information from friends in other periods to discover the exam questions ahead of time. When Berto told me about the drawing teacher's accusation, I, like him, was shocked.

ROBERTO
MORALES

Apparently another student and Berto had turned in fairly similar drawings. They were supposed to imitate a particular artist's style using a modern subject matter. Both boys selected the same model from which to work and happened to select similar subjects as well. Berto had done his project at home, and his mother had seen him laboring over it for several hours. When he told the teacher that he did not copy the other student's paper, the teacher didn't believe him. The teacher said he could not determine who copied off of whom and he would therefore offer both boys a chance to draw new pictures that would count as their final projects; if they opted not to draw the new pictures, they would receive F's. Berto was furious at the accusation and the teacher's lack of trust in him:

> I told him I didn't do it, and he didn't believe me. . . . He didn't believe in nothing [and that] got me really mad. 'Cause to not have faith in a student, it's wrong. You know, you put their self esteem down, and when he accused me of cheating, there I was, I went blank, you know. I said, "I never cheated in my life." And so he gave me one day [to redo the project], and I said, "No." I blew it off. I didn't want to do it. I didn't want to do that over again—spend five hours on a drawing, you know, and I had other homework to do also, and I couldn't do it, and my mom, even my mom said, "Don't do it because you know what you did and he doesn't know. You spent time on it at your house not at somebody else's house". . . . My mom got frustrated and my dad got frustrated 'cause never once in my life they have heard their

ROBERTO
MORALES

son cheating. . . . So my mom was there always, she was there for me. She wanted to go talk to him, but I didn't want to start no mess on it because when my mom gets involved in schoolwork, she'll really blow off her top. She's always, she backs me. . . . She loves me. I don't remember when no matter what and she'll blow off her top. . . . She doesn't care who they are; [it's] about respect because they disrespected her own son.

Roberto believes he would have had at least a B in the class had he not been falsely accused. The teacher originally said the drawing was "great," and even Berto's peers agreed it was his best work. They argued on his behalf, attempting to prove his innocence in some way, but the stipulation had already been set. Berto received an F on his final project and a C in the class overall. He was supposed to take drawing II in the spring semester but decided against it. He didn't want to take a class where the teacher did not trust him.

Unlike Michelle who, when faced with the crisis surrounding the Community class, relied on the support of her parents and school officials who knew her well, Berto opted not to enlist his parents or teachers for help. He did not consider asking Ms. Evans to intervene, nor did he want his mother to get involved even though he knew she trusted him. He wanted to "just forget the whole thing." Doing another drawing would be the same to Berto as admitting guilt, and though his decision affected his grade point average, he believed a higher grade "wasn't worth it." He knew he had done good, honest work, and that was enough for him. He saw no other feasible options and didn't understand why "these things kept happening to [him]." He simply tried to work hard and live honestly, and he felt thwarted every step of the way. One may speculate that another student, Eve, for example, would have never been accused. She had a school-wide reputation as an excellent and trustworthy

student. Though Berto was well-liked and trusted by many of his
teachers, it seems clear that this particular teacher did not know
him in this way. The hectic pace of the school day discourages
close relationships between students and teachers, and Berto and
his drawing teacher were no exception.

ROBERTO
MORALES

Similarly, the system discourages caring dialogue between teachers and students that might have resulted in very different consequences here.[4] Perhaps, if the teacher had engaged in a dialogue
with both boys, he would have discovered that the similar drawings
were actually a result of coincidence instead of cheating. Especially
with an assignment in an art class where one was *supposed* to be
imitating models, the accusation of cheating seems misplaced. The
nature of success in schools, even in art classes that often rely on
peer critique and group efforts, still predominately requires independent work and individual assessment. One could hardly imagine students of Monet, for instance, being accused of cheating as
they try to emulate the master, but in this case, even in the act of
imitation, the teacher felt obligated to treat the drawing assignment
as a sort of test, to be completed alone, for a grade. Another sad consequence is that Berto liked the drawing class and had planned to
continue. The teacher's reaction quashed his interest in the subject,
perhaps permanently, as Berto had no plans to take any other art
courses at the school.

Finally, the incident serves as an important example of the way
schools fail to reward, and in some way discourage, good behavior
on the part of the students. When so much emphasis is placed on
grades and individual achievement, the system seems to breed dis-
honesty. Students learn to succeed by all means possible, even if this
means compromising their integrity to obtain high grades. In this
sense, Berto lacks the knowledge (Bourdieu [1977] for instance,
might say the cultural capital) to succeed in the way he wishes in

school. He respects his teachers and does not question their authority, even when they may be wrong. He believes in honest
work and diligence, even when this may cause him to get lower
grades than those who cheat and procrastinate. And he believes in
helping others and receiving help in return, even when the system
is largely based on independent work and assessment. At the end of
the year, however, Berto shows some signs of wearing down; the
pressure to do well and to go to college overwhelms him, and he is
tempted to break some rules.

Stress

In May, when the weather was gloriously sunny and classes were
winding down, Roberto began to fall behind in his school work and
to do more assignments at the last minute. In S.O.S. tutorial he
rushed to complete a worksheet due that day in biology. He studied for a Spanish quiz minutes before the bell rang instead of preparing diligently the night before. And he spent most of English
class flirting with the girls behind him, ignoring the teacher's warnings to "quiet down and get to work." He still paid more attention
than most of the students in his classes and was able to answer
questions when called upon, but his grades were dropping. He received a C− on a fairly easy assignment in health—the lowest
grade he had ever received in the class.

Berto knew he was lagging. He told me he was having trouble
concentrating. He was worried about finals and about next year's
schedule. He was concerned about studying for the SATs. He had
doubts about getting into Berkeley. He even pasted the UC Berkeley handout he received from Ms. Evans on the front of his note-
book to motivate himself. Summer was so close he could taste it,
but he had to hold on for a few more weeks. The pressure contin-

ued to mount, however, and Berto, in his words, was "freak-
ing out."

In Spanish class he suddenly grew tired of helping his peers.
He told me that the class was reviewing vocabulary words for the
final exam when he "just got frustrated." With several students
standing around his desk, asking him questions and waiting for
help, he screamed, "Shut up! There's a teacher here, that's why they
pay him. They don't pay me." He said he surprised himself with this
reaction, but he had had enough. He had too much to worry about
these days to help others.

In PE he had another outburst, this time in the swimming pool
while playing water polo. He didn't want to discuss it for a few
weeks, but he eventually agreed to tell the story. According to Berto,
he and another student took the game "too seriously":

> I don't know how to explain it. You had to be there. He just was
> really annoying me, and I was getting more and more mad. . . .
> It just escalated, and we started pushing each other, you know,
> and the sub asked us both to get out of the pool. Then he said,
> "Are you both OK now?" The boy said, "Yes," and he got to go
> back in the pool, and I said "No," and had to change and leave
> PE. . . . I was mad anyways. You know I needed to cool off, too.
> I realize that now, and um it was, like, it was both our faults that
> leaded to the incident. But, you know, I was more mad than any-
> thing, and it was raining that day so it was, like, some way it
> cooled me down, the rain, . . . but I was, like, really fierced up.
> It's like when I even got into the locker room I was by myself, I
> pressed the locker so hard I left a dent. And everybody heard,
> everybody heard. . . . It was, like, I took it out, you know, I don't
> like taking it out on people.

ROBERTO
MORALES

I put it behind me, you know. It's over, it's like that wasn't important to think about any more. Everybody said, "Come on, you gonna go fight, you have to." I was like pphhhh. "You go fight them for me if you want to. . . ." I really don't care if he said I was chicken or whatever. . . . I said some things I was ashamed of, but I can tell you honestly I have never fought in my life. I took classes like karate and stuff so I can defend myself but I wouldn't know the first thing about fighting in that situation.

Similar to when Kevin destroyed the wall in the gymnasium, Berto was so angry he felt he had to release it somewhere. He chose to hit the locker instead of the boy, but the weeks following the argument were tense for him. He walked quickly through the halls, worried about confronting the student, and even on the last day of school, he told me he was "keeping [his] eyes open [for the boy], you know, just in case." He could have played the situation differently, told the substitute teacher that he had calmed down, and perhaps he would have been allowed to finish the game. But he was too upset. He found that he was quick to anger these days and that sometimes he would go home and "just break out in tears" because he was "so stressed out."

The stress increased until it was time for his final exams. By then Berto was so anxious that he became physically ill over the thought of taking the tests. Before the biology final he stayed in the bathroom for more than 30 minutes, feeling as though he might vomit. He brought a chair in and sat down next to the toilet, attempting to calm his nerves. The walk to school made him feel a little better, but when he arrived at the classroom he felt faint. Afterwards, he was sure he had done poorly.

The math final proved just as devastating, and a few days later Berto admitted that he had violated one of his cardinal rules. He changed an answer on his test after glancing at another student's exam; he had cheated, and he felt terrible. The teacher had asked Berto to put the completed exams in alphabetical order, and Berto agreed, used to doing such favors for others. When he noticed his exam and compared it to that of a "really smart student," Berto panicked:

ROBERTO
MORALES

> I was looking and I, like, counted the ones I got wrong off of his, and then I calculated and then I said, "Oh my God I got an F on this." And I was like, should I change it? I go, "Wow but I shouldn't," but I changed only one. I was like I'm just going to change one and that's it. You know, like 'cause I don't know, I don't know if he got something wrong also.

> I mean I won't feel good about that. It's like, it's wrong and what happens if I did get caught? It's like oh my God I would just fail that test automatically. Then I said, "No I can't do it." And you know, even my friends were all around [saying] "Don't do it, you can't do it." And then they were all looking at me like really weird, and I was like shoot . . . they just saw me change the one, and I was like "Nah, I shouldn't do it anymore." . . . So it was just that one, and, I feel really bad. I can't believe I did it.

Aware that the teacher usually composed five different versions of his tests to distribute to students in order to prevent cheating, I ask Berto how he knew that the student whose paper he copied was using the same exam? He said he couldn't be sure ("the answer patterns looked similar"), but he believed "the teacher said [there were different tests] to psyche everybody out." Berto thought there was only one exam, and, already upset about his transgression, he now had the extra burden of wondering whether he had cheated "correctly," or whether he had in fact changed an answer based on the wrong test. Similar to Teresa who erroneously erased the tardy marks in Spanish class, Berto was not savvy in the art of cheating. He told me that his stomach ached and that he hoped he would never feel the need to cheat again. Knowing the school system, I thought it was unlikely he would get his wish—especially given the pressure he felt to get into college.

In one sense, the S.O.S. course helped Berto with the college application process immensely, guiding him through the kinds of courses to take, informing him about requirements like the SATs, and offering resources such as tutoring, counseling, and financial aid information—benefits not usually accessible to students like Berto whose parents had no postsecondary education.[5] By focusing on the application process and arranging visits to local universities, however, the course also placed pressure on the students to get the high grades required for admission to these schools. Berto now knew that the possibility of getting into college was real, and he worried that he would let everyone down, including himself, if he failed to achieve this goal.

The stress in his life originated from other sources as well. He told me that his parents had been fighting intensely for the past few months and that he worried about the possibility of a divorce. He felt "caught in the middle" and began to "resent living at home." The night before his math final, Berto's parents had an argument and looked to Berto to mediate. He was very worried about math and felt unable to help with his parents' problems. Ultimately, he took his books and stayed overnight at his cousin's house, frustrated that his parents were so angry with one another and unhappy about missing valuable study time. He believed the constant fighting had affected both his school work and his relationship with the people who were his "greatest support":

They think I just have all this free time just to listen to them, and I don't. . . . I mean I can't live with them the way they are 'cause one minute they're together, the next minute, they're not. One minute they're together, the next day they're fighting. And then I get mad because they come to me and tell me and everything, and it sounds like they want to get a divorce but they don't do it. . . . It's like, I just can't live with them. . . .

ROBERTO MORALES

And if they go through a divorce, there goes my life, you know. . . . I can't stand losing my mother or my father because even though they annoy me, they're a big role in my life.

Though any of these pressures—final exams, parental fighting, college admissions, fear of retribution from the water polo fight, lack of time or quiet space in which to work—might have caused a student to modify his usual classroom behavior, the combination of pressures for Berto was overwhelming. As with many of the other students in this study, however, few school people seemed to notice the changes in Berto, and no one knew the extent of his suffering. He finished the year exhausted and defeated, without a 4.0 grade point average, and with little hope that the following year would get any easier.

"Fun"

In our final interview, after spending considerable time discussing the end-of-the-year changes in his behavior, I ask Berto if there is anything else he wants me to know, anything else he wants to tell me about his school experience. He replies, "Yeah. Um, I mean, to me, school's fun." When I ask him to elaborate, he stammers and says he cannot explain, but a close look at some of my field notes reveals moments where it is clear that Berto is enjoying himself in school. He takes pleasure in helping others, in tutoring his young first grader, in singing and laughing with his friends, and in moments like the one below where he gets swept away by the excitement of a classroom activity. Though these times are rare, they exemplify a kind of fleeting engagement for Berto where he is so engrossed in his task that he briefly forgets time and space:[6]

Berto is participating in a biology lab where students are looking under microscopes to search for evidence of life in marsh water. His partner looks quickly and begins cracking jokes, "Look, it's a devil; here's the horns and here's the tail." Berto doesn't appear to be listening, he is so intent on doing the lab correctly. He calls the teacher over to help them locate the correct spot on the slide, and he asks, "Mr. T, is this right? Is this right?" The teacher shows both boys what to look for and then makes his rounds around the class.

The boys must wait another ten minutes for him to return. The lab partner goes outside to chat with friends. Berto is frustrated. He says loudly, three times, "Mr. T, Mr. T," almost screaming the last time, "Mister T!" Finally the teacher comes over and helps. Berto says, "Oh man, we had one [a good find on the slide] but now it's gone!" The teacher looks and says enthusiastically, "This is great! You have a spirogyra!" Berto looks and gets excited: "It's swimming fast! Oh man, now it's gone. I lost it [he pretends to sob exaggeratedly]; it's probably dead." He continues to search for it for a few more minutes, then looks up to find the teacher gone and his partner still at the door. He glances at the clock and says "Oh well, time to clean up."

Though there is evidence of some changed behavior here near the end of the semester—the way Berto yells to get the teacher's attention, for instance—Berto still seems to exemplify a diligence and positive attitude toward learning that distinguishes him from many of the other students in the class. He wants to get the assignment right and to find evidence of marsh life, so much so that when he discovers a good specimen, he genuinely becomes excited. The teacher shares Berto's enthusiasm and congratulates him on his success, but when the teacher leaves to help another group, Berto is still involved with the moment. He has no idea that the other students are cleaning up and beginning to write their reports. Nor does he realize that he is the only student who showed (outwardly, at least) some sign of emotion at this discovery. Surely, other students found spirogyra under their microscopes, but most simply recorded the event in their notebooks and moved on to the next task. Berto briefly engaged with the material and enjoyed himself in the process. Then, just as quickly, he snapped back to the reality of classroom life and focused on the lab write-up, the part of the assignment that would be graded and therefore mattered more than the engagement.

I am reminded of the classroom sign I describe in Chapter 1 about Faircrest's values. Berto, even through the difficult month of May, embodied almost all of these: He did his homework on time, showed a desire to learn, paid attention and participated in class, respected teachers and other students, cared about his future, and always tried his best. And yet these qualities, along with his integrity and generosity, did not allow him to achieve his desired grade point average. In some cases, his diligence and honesty served as obstacles to his success. Like the other students in this study who felt the need to compromise their beliefs or ideals in the course of doing school, Berto too gave in at times to impulses to act rudely, to cheat, and to stop helping others when the pressure was great. However, he also showed a kind of naiveté about the workings of

ROBERTO
MORALES

the school system. Unlike the others who discovered ways to manipulate school processes to aid them in their pursuits, Berto never acquired this school-savvy. Instead, he vowed to work "even harder" next year and hoped that his "spirit" and belief in himself would "see [him] through." He did not realize that in order to achieve the success he aspired, he would have to work "smarter" in addition to harder.

CHAPTER 7

The Predicament of "Doing School"

If you learn how to manipulate the system, then you learn how you can survive in high school without going nuts.
—Michelle Spence

This is just my work style. . . . This is how I do school.
—Eve Lin

The school guidance counselor believes Kevin, Eve, Michelle, Teresa, and Berto represent Faircrest's "best and brightest." The history department chair wishes he had a class full of students like these. They seem to be diligent, talented, and focused. They get good grades,[1] win awards and commendations, pursue extracurricular interests, do community service, and help teachers and administrators at the school. But in pursuit of this success, the students participate in behavior of which they are not proud. They learn to cheat, kiss up, form treaties, contest school decisions, and act in ways that run counter to explicit or implicit school rules and guidelines. Often their behavior contradicts the very traits and values many parents, students, and community members expect schools to instill.

By rewarding certain kinds of success above others, Faircrest High may actually impede that which it hopes to achieve. Instead of fostering in its students traits such as honesty, integrity, cooperation, and respect, the school may be promoting deception, hostility, and anxiety.

Why must the students feel the need to manipulate the system and devise crafty strategies to get ahead? Why must they feel compelled to betray friends and deceive teachers? Why must they compromise integrity for future success? In this chapter, I explore the conditions and consequences of pursuing school success and the persistent dilemmas faced by those in the school system: What exactly is being learned in high schools like Faircrest? And at what costs?

"Doing School"

The students depicted here do in a sense represent Faircrest's "best and brightest." Having cleverly determined what kind of behavior gets rewarded in school, they have devoted themselves to pursuing strategies that lead to this kind of success. Each of the students, to varying degrees and some more consciously than others, learns to manage the workload through a variety of techniques:

Establishing allies and treaties. The school world has been described as a place where, too often, students feel anonymous and powerless.[2] Yet, the students in this study, either by deliberate "kissing up" or by the nature of their courses, relationships, and activities at the school, were fortunate to discover people who knew them personally and who could intervene on their behalf.[3] The adults served as advocates and allies for the students, willing to listen to their complaints, form treaties, offer their trust, and bestow kindness in various ways. While most of these adults still only knew certain aspects about the students' school and home lives, the little information they did know seemed to benefit the students. Without the understanding and support of these adults, the students might not have fared as well as they did.[4]

Multi-tasking. Just as teachers practice classroom management techniques to "control" students, most of these students devised their own form of classroom management to control the workload. For instance, all but Berto practiced multi-tasking, a term borrowed from the business world that means to work simultaneously on a variety of tasks. Efficiency experts advise busy executives to maximize their time by doing routine tasks such as going through the mail or signing purchase orders while speaking on the phone or attending meetings. Effective multi-taskers at Faircrest surreptitiously worked on French homework during math class, memorized lines for drama while watching a movie in history, and studied for a physics test while pretending to pay attention in English class. They understood the need to appear well-prepared and on-task, even if they were not, sometimes going as far as to photocopy textbook pages to minimize the chances of being caught with the wrong book open on the desk. Some, like Teresa and Michelle, established treaties that allowed them to multi-task freely and without guilt; others, like Eve and Kevin, devised ways to divert the teachers' attention, such as raising their hands every ten minutes to give the illusion of participating in the class discussions.

Cheating. The widespread cheating I observed represents a classroom management strategy as well. The more traditional forms of cheating—copying answers from peers' tests, plagiarizing, and relying upon forbidden aids such as cheat sheets—were used to help the students obtain high grades without spending as much time actually studying the material. For Kevin and Teresa, cheating became a habitual crutch, enabling them to "do the minimum to get by," even if the results were less than satisfactory. Some of the more creative forms of what might be called cheating—"winging it" in class discussions and oral presentations, "ditching" class on test days to find extra time to study, relying on friends to work "cooperatively" on assignments that should be done independently—all represent further time-saving, grade-enhancing devices. Students like Eve and Kevin learned how to employ these strategies wisely; they knew how to hide their deception and in which classrooms these practices were tacitly allowed.

"Squeaky Wheels." At times, these forms of classroom management required rather aggressive behavior on the part of the students. All but Berto chose to contest a teacher's grading decision during the semester. Kevin regularly voiced dissent over marked errors on tests and quizzes, often resulting in a change to a higher grade. Teresa, Eve, and Michelle approached the school principal on separate occasions to complain about teaching styles or administrative decisions. To Berto, who refused to contest his drawing teacher's decision and opted instead for a lower grade, such tactics may have seemed drastic and disrespectful, but for the others, these strategies were a necessary part of finessing the system. With so many students and so many bureaucratic hurdles in the school institution, only the students who made themselves known, who spoke up and questioned authority, got heard. Even if the student's performance did not necessarily warrant an extra point or a higher grade, complaining loudly, strongly, and regularly was thought to yield slightly better results, especially since teachers were strapped for time and the assessments they conducted were usually influ-

enced by a variety of factors, including how much the student appeared to care about the work being done.

These management strategies, though effective in most cases for leading to high grades and status at the school, also led to anxiety and frustration. The students did not like competing with their peers, acting deceptively toward friends and adults, or compromising their values. They did not like the lifestyles they had to adopt in order to succeed or the sacrifices they needed to make. But they also did not feel as if they had a choice in the matter.

The Grade Trap

On the one hand, the students believed that they needed to achieve high grades, high test scores, and various honors in order to secure future success—usually in the form of an advanced degree and a high-paying job. As Eve said, "That's all I can think about . . . to get in [to an Ivy League School] and become a successful $500,000-a-year doctor or engineer or whatever it is I want to be." Though uncertain about the exact profession she hoped to enter, she was sure of her ultimate goal. She wanted to be wealthy and to be able to live in the manner to which she had grown accustomed. Kevin, Teresa, and Roberto also specifically mentioned the financial benefits they believed would result from a college degree. And, in one sense, they were correct in their assumptions. Job prospects are better for college graduates as compared to high school graduates, and wages tend to go up with increased schooling. Furthermore, since more students are pursuing higher education these days, a credential from a more prestigious university may lead to higher income and job security than a degree from a college considered to have lower standards for admission or fewer academic resources available to students.[5] As long as the employment market continues to value certain credentials over others, these students see the utility of pursuing admission to a reputable university and of devoting their high school careers toward achieving this goal.

On the other hand, the students also wanted to feel good about themselves and their achievements. They wanted to believe that they deserved their high grades and status and that they had earned their success. They tried to justify their behavior, convince themselves that they were doing "the right thing," or that "everybody" did school this way. But they could not escape the fact that they were unhappy with their school decisions and were not content with what they believed were the limited options available to them. Most said that they wanted to "concentrate on learning," not worry about grades, act in ways that were authentic and did not compromise their beliefs. They did not like "manipulating the system" or "playing the game," and they especially did not like the sacrifices they felt obligated to make in the name of grades.

As Eve said, "This school turns students into robots . . . just going page by page, doing the work, doing the routine." She and the others lamented the fact that school was "lifeless." Passion and engagement were rare, and the daily grind of the school day took its toll on their "health and happiness." Most were unable to find a way to succeed in school and still, in their words, "have a life." They longed to find a balance between work and play. They wanted to resist the pull of the system turning them into "high school machines," or robo-students, drudgingly pursuing high marks without necessarily learning the material.

Though adolescents have been typically characterized as having too much free time on their hands and of being overly concerned with leisure activities and social life,[6] the students in this study defied the stereotypes. Their school days started early, a full hour or two before most adults began their work days, and often ended late at night, after soccer practice, dance rehearsals, student council meetings, paid job responsibilities, and homework time. Some of the students, like Teresa and Michelle, suffered frequent colds and illnesses due to such a harried pace, a lack of sleep, and poor eating habits. Others, like Eve and Berto, who studied "every minute," experienced great stress that led to anxiety, stomach problems, even a possible ulcer (for Eve). These students wished they could get more hours of sleep and improve their health, but their busy schedules, including school, family, and work obligations, did not allow this change. Similarly, they wished they could spend more time with friends, pursue other activities, or take a few days off, but most believed they could not do these things and still maintain their high grades. They recognized that they needed to make a choice, and for them, future success was more important than present happiness.

The students also complained about a system that appeared to show little support for intellectual engagement and passion. They studied the material, read the textbooks, and completed the assignments, for the most part, because they had to, not because they wanted to or because the subjects genuinely interested them. Students often memorized facts and figures without stopping to ask what they meant, or why they were asked to learn the facts in the first place. They selected courses based on college requirements and grade transcripts and reluctantly accepted the curricula in these courses as beyond their control. Michelle, for example, was frustrated that individual subjects were taught in "bits and pieces," where teachers made virtually no efforts to connect U.S. history and American literature, for instance, with topics she was studying in drama or psychology.

Eve admitted that any content area knowledge she gained along the way was largely incidental. Once she took an exam, she said most of the facts she had memorized "emptied out of [her] brain." She was required to move on to the next assignment to keep up with the pace of the class. Taking time to reflect or to engage with the material would only slow her down and adversely affect her grades. Thus, students generally went from class to class, routinely performing assignments and having little time to debrief or think about what they had just "learned."[7] For the most part, they were asked to accumulate facts that seemed to have little relevance to their lives and to complete tasks accurately and efficiently without delving deeply into subjects. An A grade, therefore, did not necessarily mean that the students learned and retained content area knowledge and skills or that they understood important concepts or theories; rather, the grades proved that the students were adept at providing the teachers with the information required on tests and quizzes, and that they had memorized these facts and figures (or copied them from peers) just long enough to "ace" the exams and then move on to the next set of tasks.

If the students weren't learning the intended curriculum at the school, if they weren't gaining a deep understanding of the subject matter of their courses, then what exactly were they learning? As Eve described it, "high school is a way of building up a tolerance for stress" and only the most "fit" survive. This reference to a Darwinian survival system seems apt. Successful students learned to devise various strategies to stay ahead of their peers and to please those in power positions; unsuccessful students, for a variety of reasons, were not as adept at playing the survival game. They ultimately received low grades and were weeded out of the competition for higher credentials.[8] The students recognized that despite the school's rhetoric of wanting to "help each student reach his or her goals," not every student would be able to succeed. Only so many students could comprise the top 15 percent of the class admitted to the honors level courses. For every top 15, there is a "bottom" 85 percent; thus, academic success for some—as sanctioned by Faircrest

High—must necessarily be accompanied by academic failure for others. And as Varenne and McDermott (1998) attest in their book *Successful Failure*, this is the way it is in most American schools.

Constraints of the School System

The school system is constructed for only a few to "succeed." And many of us have become so used to this model that we can hardly see the problems inherent in it. Students and adults in this study are influenced by and help to shape the culture of the school. They adapt their behaviors in light of the larger school system. The students who are considered to be successful in this culture represent what I call effective "classroom chameleons."

Student adaptations. Like chameleons who use dramatic color changes to camouflage themselves in order to stay alive, the successful students at Faircrest exhibited vastly different behaviors from class to class in order to meet the diverse expectations of their teachers. For example, Kevin acted like a clown in French class, joking with the teacher and acting as a cheerleader for his peers, while he behaved as a serious and fierce competitor in PE class. Michelle, too, behaved one way in her drama class, often acting more like a teacher's assistant, but she preferred to keep to herself and to work at her own pace in her math and history courses, establishing treaties in order to spend class time working on other assignments. In each case, the students were rewarded for their various actions—though their successful behavior in one course looked very different from the behaviors they exhibited in the others.

This quality of adaptability, to change one's "colors" to please various teachers, served the students well. Not only did they learn to provide general depictions of success, such as raising their hands even when they didn't know the answers, many of the students learned to read and provide particular depictions for each of their classroom teachers. Figuring out how to "play the game" effectively in high school is difficult in and of itself, but figuring out six or seven different games, and then adapting classroom behaviors to play them all well, is extremely challenging.

Heath and McLaughlin (1993) argue that youth need to learn how to behave successfully in a variety of contexts in order to survive the transitions from adolescence to adulthood and from school to work. Others who support this view assert the need for resources such as economic, social, and cultural "capital" to help promote successful transitions. They note that the inequities that exist in our communities today prevent certain youth from achieving school success.[9]

It is clear that the adolescents in this study benefited from resources not available to all youth. Most had supportive and caring parents who saw that basic needs of food, shelter, clothing, and safety were met. These parents intervened on behalf of the students and found various ways to show support for their children's education, such as helping them achieve access to special classes, vouching for the students in meetings with teachers and administrators, and even dismissing "unexcused" absences. In this sense, the parents also learned to "do school" successfully, serving as allies and playing an important role in promoting their children's futures.

Many of the students also had access to other adults, such as teachers and relatives, who encouraged the value of education and who could provide information about colleges and admissions requirements. Most of the students had strong literacy skills (Teresa is an exception here) to comprehend and portray depictions of success, and had positive early education experiences in which they could practice these techniques. In addition, all of the students in this study believed they had a likely promise of a future to aspire toward, one which they had the power to help shape.[10]

Eve and Kevin, both of whom came from higher socioeconomic backgrounds than the other three students, were fortunate in that they had a few more resources available to them: they could choose to focus their energy on schoolwork and extracurriculars without the pressures and responsibilities of working at a paid job for 20 or more hours each week. They had study aids such as individual, quiet spaces to do homework; their own computers, printers, and modems; and enough money to afford to pay for books, classes, and fees associated with AP and SAT exams that would help them gain admission to good colleges. Berto and Teresa (and to some extent Michelle), did not have access to these kinds of resources, and, consequently, this lack impacted their school experiences and limited their options.[11]

Though the five students described here differed in their understanding of teacher and classroom expectations, and in how they adapted to contextual clues, all relied on some economic, social, and cultural capital to help them "fit in" to the school environment and experience success. The students were fortunate (to varying degrees) both to have access to resources that helped them adapt and to be savvy enough to understand how to use these benefits to their advantage.

Along with the benefits of adaptability, however, come some costs. The students who change their behavior to fit certain situations also face anonymity and the problems associated with it. No one knows the "true" colors of the chameleon, and no single teacher or administrator may know the "whole" student or the complexities of his or her school life. Teresa, for example, exhibited some of the most varied behaviors of all the students in the study. In her business courses her actions led to the Outstanding Business Student award; she was quiet and well-behaved, turned in work on time, and completed the "easy" assignments with very few mistakes.

In science and Spanish classes, however, Teresa was frequently absent. She regularly failed to complete assignments, came to class unprepared, and appeared to lack an interest in the subjects. (She was actually interested in the topics taught in biology, but her home obligations and language problems caused her to fall behind and do poorly.) Because of this disparity in the way she performed, some teachers considered her a model student while others regarded her as unsuccessful. Her Spanish teacher said to me early on, "[Teresa] will probably fail this course. Why don't you write about some of my successful students?"

The Spanish teacher here had no way of knowing that Teresa was considered one of the most successful students in the business program. She assumed that Teresa's behavior in language class was consistent with her behavior in other classes. Nor did she comprehend the reasons behind Teresa's actions. She did not ask about Teresa's home life or her job responsibilities (and even if she had, it is not clear whether Teresa would have answered her sufficiently), she did not ask about her workload in other courses, or her anxiety and frustration about having "a future." The school structure was not set up for this teacher to get to know these aspects of Teresa's life. She had 50 minutes a day to teach an intensive Spanish curriculum, and because of her limited access to the students and her large classes, because she worked mostly in isolation from the other teachers in the school due to the departmental structure, and because she had no reason to ask to see Teresa's transcripts or grades in other courses (this was considered to be the business of counselors, those responsible for the "whole" student), she could not easily get to know Teresa in a way that might have benefited her as a student. Without understanding the complexity of Teresa's life, the Spanish teacher based her assessment of Teresa on the behaviors she witnessed each day in her first-period class.

Teacher adaptations. The same could be said for most of the other teachers in this study. Like the blind men who argue over the description of the elephant because they each have access to only one component of the animal, high school teachers at Faircrest and schools like it are blind to many aspects of their students' lives. Most see only one side of the student, often a camouflage designed to conceal an identity in order to blend in with the teacher's expectations. The students may use the disguises to hide their weaknesses or to show off their strengths, but in either case, the teacher is privy to only a partial view, often resulting in a lack of useful knowledge about the students, or worse, misconstructions about the youth. This incomplete picture of a student may be one reason why Roberto was falsely accused of cheating by his drawing teacher, or why his Spanish teacher incorrectly believed that he was lazy. It may also explain why his math teacher did not know about his severe test anxiety. Had the teacher known about Berto's fear of exams, he might have offered a different entrance requirement for the honors course. As Michelle said when Richard accused her of foul play after leaving The Community Project, "I can't believe he said I was trying to get away with something! Anyone who knows me, knows this is just not me." The trouble is Richard did not know Michelle, at least not well enough to trust her, and this lack of knowledge and trust led to great misunderstanding.

Though a close examination of teacher adaptations is beyond the scope of this study, throughout the semester I couldn't help but notice that the teachers seemed to struggle with many of the same dilemmas faced by their students. They, too, seemed trapped by the realities of an overcrowded, impersonal, bureaucratic, and competitive school system. There were too many students to get to know, too many individual needs to be met, and too little time, money, or support from administrators to accomplish these goals.[12] For many of the teachers, like the students they taught, it was difficult enough to make it through the hectic pace of the school day—to keep order in their classrooms; to "cover" the lessons, texts, and materials required of them; to fulfill a myriad of clerical responsibilities; and to negotiate the hassles associated with department and school policies and politics, let alone strive to help each student reach his or her individual goals.

Some were forced in certain ways to be "robo-teachers," appearing to go through the motions of planning lessons, giving lectures, and grading papers in order to keep up with the overwhelming responsibilities associated with their jobs. Too much time on any one task or with any particular student could throw off the schedule for an entire week. Each moment in the school day was critical, and I noticed that teachers tended to multi-task like their students to save valuable time. For instance, they would grade homework and tests while showing films or while students participated in small group work, and they would hold student conferences during the first few minutes of class time. They would also cut corners by assigning less homework (see Kevin's chemistry teacher, Chapter 2), relying upon standardized tests from the textbooks, or eliminating short answers or essays on exams which invariably were more difficult and time-consuming to grade. Like their students, the faculty appeared to suffer from stress and burnout. They, too, faced pressures to produce high test scores and to help students get admitted to top colleges. Though one can imagine that many of these teachers entered the profession to enlighten students, to spark an excitement for inquiry and a passion for certain subject areas, most faced the reality of the grade trap where fostering student engagement was subsumed by a need to "cover" certain material, to get students to pass exams, and to find efficient ways to compensate for overbearing workloads.

Even the counselors who were supposed to act on behalf of each student's best interests felt compelled to advise students to "go for the grades" rather than learn the material in depth. Kevin's counselor, for instance, told him to switch language courses from French to Latin during his junior year in order to get his grades up, regardless of Kevin's interests in the language or his several years of studying French. Though the counselors are often the only adults at the school who have some knowledge of the students' home and work lives, have access to all course grades and transcripts, and may therefore be in a position to care for each individual and help meet specific needs, they, too, must balance competing demands. At Faircrest, the counselors met with students only twice a year for 20 minutes. None of the students in this study discussed any personal matters with their counselors, nor did they have an opportunity to reflect on their lives as students or talk about the frustrations they felt as a result of the curriculum. Though the counselors may have wanted to help students in this way, their tight schedules and orientation toward college admissions prevented them from doing so.

School constraints. The factors that wield direct influence over students and adults at the school seem especially powerful when one considers how long they have been around. Though school policies fluctuate over time, historians such as Tyack and Cuban (1995) note a persistent consistency in school classrooms and explain this "grammar of schooling" as due to a lack of effective reform efforts to bring about fundamental educational change.

Hence, many of the school factors discussed in this chapter remain largely the same today as they did years ago. For instance, several specific characteristics of the school structure continue to influence the way students do school. The fragmented school day is divided into six or seven classes that take place in 50-minute chunks with few breaks or free periods. The large class sizes and teacher and counselor overload lead to treaties, compromises, and student anonymity. The tracking system, with its focus on preparation for college, gives students in the basic (or lower) tracks fewer course options and limited ability to switch tracks, and reserves honors/ AP courses for students in the top 15 percent of their class. The departmental organization by subject area may contribute to a fragmented curriculum, limited interdisciplinary studies, and eventual teacher and student isolation.

Despite policy shifts and some changes in course offerings, the high school curriculum has also remained virtually the same over the past few decades[13] and leads students and teachers alike to adapt their behavior in the particular ways described above. When a course curriculum is divided into discrete units and tasks with little cohesion between units, and when the emphasis is on learning facts and techniques as opposed to problem-solving skills or deep understanding of fundamental themes and theories, it is no wonder that students pursue tasks with a robot-like mentality and show little interest in or engagement with the material. There is little time built-in to the curriculum for reflection or de-briefing, so students tend to plod ahead to the next assignment without much attention to the larger picture. Similarly, when most of the honors and advanced placement curricula are based on college models where certain material must be covered to prepare for year-end exams, students tend to focus on the end results—getting the grades and passing the tests. The students believe that the curriculum is not relevant to their lives or useful in the "real world." They complain that teachers fail to solicit their input and do not design curricula to meet pupils' desires, interests, needs, and passions.

Finally, since the late 1800s, high schools have relied upon grades, test scores, and class rankings to assess student achievement.[14] At

Faircrest, these measures lead to outcome-oriented teaching and learning, memorization and regurgitation of material, and a lack of deep understanding of the concepts being taught. The focus on grades and scores encourages extrinsic motivation and a culture of competition. It also tends to privilege certain student competencies over others, as the frequent use of tests or quizzes emphasizes verbal or mathematical abilities, and fails to hold students accountable for developing other vital skills and techniques. Individual student achievement is promoted over the value of cooperation and group success, especially through the use of class curves and other strategies that limit the number of students who can achieve high grades. Even the monthly departmental awards, honors bulletin boards, AP score banners, and other forms of public recognition at the school may promote individual achievement in ways that are more harmful than celebratory.[15] These "messages" of what it means to be successful at the school, along with brochures and course guides that emphasize honors courses, college attendance, and high test scores, seem to ignite feelings of intense competition.

As McDermott (1993) notes, students cannot be successful or unsuccessful alone—everyone (parents, teachers, counselors, and so on) is part of the choreography that produces moments for degradation or praise. These dilemmas and adaptations that the students and school adults experience in the name of "getting the grades" appear to go well beyond the schools. The students who compete with each other for top grades in high school, and later, top grades in college, will eventually compete for top jobs and salaries outside of school. Thus, the behaviors I describe here do not occur in a vacuum. Many of the forces that contribute to the adaptations that the students call "doing school" take place within the schools themselves and are reactions to or consequences of existing school structure, curriculum, and assessment factors. However, these school factors are also influenced by (and help to shape) a complex medley of forces from the larger community and from the national culture.

We Get What We Bargain For

The push toward high grades, top scores, and college attendance is not unique to Faircrest High School. Indeed, the extreme wealth of much of the community and the high level of economic and professional success of many of its members spurs an ideology of achievement, perpetuated by parents, businesses, colleges, media, and other sources.[16] In the town of Faircrest, housing prices are well above the national norm, in part because people are willing to pay a premium for its distinguished public schools. Town papers advertise special prenatal classes for expectant mothers to improve the intelligence quotients of the unborn children. Parents put infants on long waiting lists for preschools with reputations for academic excellence, and they camp out overnight to win spots in the elementary schools with the highest test scores. The messages of academic success can be heard long before high school, as students vie for top classes in sixth and seventh grades and take practice PSAT tests as young as age ten.

People in Faircrest and places like it seem to have become obsessed with "being the best" and helping their children acquire top credentials. The drive to succeed has led some parents to employ expensive agencies to tutor their children to get high scores on the SATs. Kevin's father insisted that Kevin go through the tutoring program a second time when he missed his goal of a combined score of 1200 by 50 points. Kevin did not believe 50 points would significantly hurt his chances for admission to the University of California, but his father was adamant. Other families turned to

Web sites that sold high-priced college application essays "guaranteed" to get students into Ivy League universities.

At a gathering of local third graders, Faircrest children speak in earnest of their hopes to attend Stanford or Harvard when they grow up. In part, the children say this because their parents attended these schools, or their parents have told them to strive for acceptance to these kinds of schools, and they learn to equate credentials from prestigious universities with status and wealth. "I want to be rich and drive a Lexus," one youngster remarked, "so I need to get A's." They want to go to Harvard or Stanford in order to gain material success—not, it seems, to pursue a love of knowledge and learning. Few recognize the reality: The majority of them will not be admitted to these schools, and their focus on grades and transcripts may be setting them up for future failure.

The idea that good grades will eventually lead to great riches may be documented at the national level as well. A recent study by the American Council on Education shows that the number one goal for 74 percent of college freshmen is to be "very well off financially." This attitude represents a shift since 1967, when 82 percent of entering students said their primary concern was to "develop a meaningful philosophy of life." The study also reported that more college freshmen were being admitted with high school grade point averages of 3.8 or better and that students today tended to be more "practical and grade grubbing."[17]

Faircrest, then, is not unusual in being a place where students dream of becoming rich via the path of academic success, and where parents and others perpetuate an achievement ideology and race for credentials beginning at a very young age. Consequently, like their children and their children's teachers, the parents in this study faced several dilemmas. On the one hand, they appeared to want to encourage their children to do well in school and to strive for admission to good colleges. On the other hand, the parents did not like the consequences that sometimes accompanied this encouragement.

According to Eve, her parents worried that they had pushed her too hard. They wanted her to slow down and regain her health, but their concerns came too late and were seen by her as disingenuous. Eve was already convinced that they and she would not be happy with anything less than an acceptance to an Ivy League institution. Kevin and Berto tell similar stories. They experienced great frustration as they attempted to meet their parents' expectations for success.[18]

What were these parents to do? One can imagine that these adults wanted their children to feel fulfilled in school, to learn the material without cheating or compromising their beliefs, and to feel excited about what they were learning. But these parents also might have realized the risks involved when a student chooses, for example, to spend all her time on drama at the expense of other subjects. Or when she refuses to conform to teacher expectations on written assignments, opting instead to follow personal preferences. (Or when, perhaps, she decides that it is more valuable to stay home and trace the voyage of Ulysses—as educator Nel Noddings' daughter did, with her mother's support [Noddings, 1992]—than to attend classes for the week.) The students risk falling behind in their courses. They might receive low grades or poor recommendations from teachers, or they may determine, like Michelle's sister, that high school was not worth attending at all. Could the parents live with such consequences? They did not want their children to be unhappy in school, but they also did not want their children to miss out on future opportunities. They did not want to put too much pressure on them to succeed, but they did not want to be too lax with their expectations either. Like the others, the parents seemed trapped by the system's constraints.

Day after day I witnessed choices that reflected the importance of success and achievement over other, conflicting values such as honesty and integrity. In this sense, the parents, teachers, and students appear to be behaving like many successful people in other American social institutions. They recognize the need for compromises, no matter how frustrating, and they develop strategies to get ahead—strategies that seem to be as useful in the classroom as they are in the boardroom. In both arenas, people have been known to "kiss up," "pass the buck," "cover" themselves, and "appear to be in control" even if they are not. As Philip Jackson (1968/1990) wrote years ago, "Learning how to make it in school involves, in part, learning how to falsify our behavior" (p. 27), and the same might be said for learning how to make it as a business executive, a lawyer, or an American president, for that matter, all of whom set examples for young people to emulate.

One might argue that given the similarities between achieving school success and doing well in other social institutions, Faircrest and high schools like it are preparing students well for the workforce. The "best and brightest" learn to acquire skills they will use in the future, and which may indeed lead them to the lucrative careers they desire. These may not be the skills the teachers, parents, or students want to engender, but we get the schools we bargain for, no matter how unconsciously.[19] In the American capitalist system, students learn to compete; the goal is to win, "to beat the others," in Eve's words, even if this means acting in ways that are personally frustrating and dissatisfying.

One may ask, is it worth it? Are we resigned to teaching only these kinds of lessons in schools? What are the costs to our children and our communities?

Though savvy students may glean useful strategies that lead to high grades and test scores, are they acquiring the content knowledge and problem-solving skills they need to succeed in the workplace?[20] If, as the students attest, they are not learning the intended curriculum of the school in more than a superficial way, is the result that they will not be adequately prepared for college or future careers? Just what does it take to produce a thoughtful citizenry or skilled workforce? And do the student adaptations described here undermine these larger goals?

Ultimately, when the students and others in this study reflect on their behavior in and around school, they feel torn. They want to feel pride in their accomplishments and would like to convince themselves that they have earned their rewards fairly and honestly. Such rationalizations help to promote the illusion of an American meritocracy,[21] that hard work and good behavior will allow the most talented and deserving to succeed in ways the high schools sanction. Yet the students and adults alike acknowledge that merit alone—that is, knowledge of the material, good study habits, and critical thinking abilities, for instance—do not necessarily lead to high grades and admissions to top colleges. Diligence and honesty, as Berto eventually realizes, will get a student only so far, and thus, many feel compelled to turn to less honorable tactics and strategies to achieve success.

After hearing about some of the traps the students in this study experienced and the tolls of success they faced—their lack of fulfillment, their sleep and health problems, their constant anxiety and frustration—a colleague of mine shook her head and said, "I *wish* my students had some of those problems!" She explained that many of her students regularly failed their classes, rarely came to school, and showed little motivation to graduate high school or pursue further learning. This was, in effect, their way of doing school. She said she would rather her students get ulcers from working too hard than face unemployment and poverty from not working in school at all. If at one end of a continuum, the choice is to face future poverty, and at the other end is to achieve a certain kind of success but pay the tolls associated with it, I, too, would probably opt for the latter. Instead, however, I question this continuum and a system that purports such limited choices, where students don't seem to learn the intended curriculum and are not challenged or excited by their education.

When we consider the pervasive factors listed above, the university expectations, national policies, community and parental desires, and the school factors that seem so difficult to reform, we may shrug our shoulders in defeat. The system is too entrenched, too complex, and too vast to make significant changes. Yet, when we listen to what students want from their high school education, what they believe they need to be productive citizens and to feel genuinely successful, we may begin to see possible alternatives to the kinds of schools and systems of competition exemplified above.

"If Only Things Could Be Different"

When Michelle is on stage, Teresa is practicing her dance moves, or Kevin is collecting the school supplies for his community service project, these students are not thinking about grades. They are not busy watching the clock or rushing to finish the task. Nor are they necessarily preoccupied with various management strategies or system-playing.

Instead, they are extremely focused on their work, passionately committed to doing it in the best possible way, and willing to toil long hours until satisfied with the results. This sense of passion, of intrinsic motivation to complete a task well, regardless of grades or placement on college transcripts, represents one distinguishing characteristic of the kind of engagement I saw on rare occasions at the school. Most of the time, this engagement occurred during participation in an extracurricular activity. Sometimes, though, the engagement took place in an academic course, as in the case with Eve's NASA project or Berto's brief moment of discovery in the science lab. The period of engagement may have been fleeting or may have lasted several weeks as the project was completed, but in each case the student felt some excitement for the task and had a desire to do it well regardless of the grade received. In many cases the students believed the tasks were important, that they had real consequences and could make a difference for others.

When the students in this study reflect deeply on their school experiences, all wish for more moments like these, more moments of satisfaction where they feel they truly deserve the praise they receive for the tasks they accomplish. Such a notion is not new. The qualities of engagement experienced by the students in their public service, arts, or project-based activities all coincide with findings from other researchers who write about "ideal" learning experiences. They note that engaged students feel intrinsic motivation to do well, a loss of track of time, and a willingness to work extra hours. Engaging activities offer students opportunities to practice traditionally adult roles that lead to real consequences and skill development, and that students report greater feelings of efficacy and satisfaction when the tasks are completed.[22]

What the students say they want are more opportunities to do real work as opposed to game-playing. This is why Teresa does not accept the outstanding business student award. This is why Michelle transfers out of The Community Project. This is why Kevin posts the newspaper article about PenPals above his bed. These students long for what they believe is genuine, real success for jobs done well, a different kind of success from what they experience for the most part in school. They want more moments of engagement in school and, ideally, a context that supports this kind of learning.

Such places do exist—places like Michelle's elementary school where students can "let their imaginations run wild" and can "get credit for doing things that [they] love." Today, a number of schools around the country are attempting to actualize some of the visions for education described here. These are schools that have made fundamental changes in areas of curriculum, school structure, and assessment. Some have drastically reduced the number of students they serve and have lowered the student to teacher ratio in an effort to personalize education.[23] Such efforts seem critical if we are to help students find adult allies who care for them and who can help to design school programs around students' specific needs and interests.

Others have designed curricula around a small number of concepts and skills to be covered in depth, eschewing traditional subject areas and courses. They choose to organize lessons around central challenges or problems to be solved, many of which have application to the world outside of school.[24]

Other programs are changing student rules and policies to "humanize" the high school experience. Some have eliminated rigid school schedules, allowing open-ended periods for learning and encouraging ample time for students to reflect on their classroom experiences. Some schools have also eliminated certain restrictions on students, allowing them to use the restrooms whenever they feel the need, to eat and drink freely in class, and to go off campus without special permission. These schools trust students to act responsibly and understand that certain human needs must be met before students can concentrate fully on schoolwork.[25]

Alternative schools have also made significant changes in the forms of assessment they employ. Some schools have replaced the traditional grading system with a series of "mastery exhibitions,"[26] where students can demonstrate learning in a variety of ways. They may choose to perform a dramatic piece, write a report, field questions from teachers and peers, complete a project, or create other "exhibits," in an attempt to show that they have mastered the material.

These are just a few examples of some of the ways schools have made progress toward engaging students with the curriculum and serving their individual needs. The work that they have done and continue to do is admirable, but it is not enough. These alternative schools and programs still must function within the larger context of a competitive structure and a university system that relies upon traditional measures of achievement. Hence, the contextual conditions for "doing school" cannot be ignored. These conditions inevitably lead to a regression to the norm, where alternative schools remain few and far between and where, almost ninety years later, most American classrooms do not fulfill John Dewey's vision of educational experiences that lead toward growth.

On the one hand, I want to praise the attempts to create alternative schools like the ones described above, and I am buoyed by their successes. On the other hand, I have to believe that this "tinkering"[27] is not an effective route toward achieving large-scale or long-term educational reform. I believe we need a new vision of what it means to be successful in school and what it means to be successful in America. We need to ask ourselves, as Nel Noddings (1992) encourages, about the kind of education we would want for our own children and then extrapolate this to all children: to ask, for example, if the model of competition and corruption revealed in the portraits here—the grade traps and balancing acts that oblige students to become school robots or chameleons and to give up personal desires for authenticity and engagement in the name of grades and future success—represents the kind of education we would choose for own sons and daughters? Do we know what values our schools are teaching? Do we like the models of success esteemed in society today? Must we be resigned to the kind of educational experiences described here?

Teresa sighs at the end of a long school day and says, "if only things could be different." Imagine a place where Berto did not have to take tests, where he could exhibit his knowledge in a variety of ways and feel as "smart" as his peers. Imagine a place where Kevin did not feel pressure to cheat, and where projects like PenPals became a part of the intended curriculum of the school. Imagine a school where people knew about Teresa's extensive home and work obligations and where these tasks were valued and integrated with her school lessons. Imagine if Michelle did not have to choose between her love for drama and her desire to study interdisciplinary issues and concepts, and if Eve could slow down and enjoy the process of learning for learning's sake. What kinds of changes would need to be made in school policy, in colleges and university admissions criteria, in state frameworks, in course scheduling, curriculum development, and student assessment, to name a few, and in our American system overall to help make these visions possible?

Only by working closely with the high school students and by listening to their needs, frustrations, and desires may we begin to pursue answers to the important questions raised here. Without their voices, we are missing a key component of any conversation on school success.

Epilogue

Nearly three years have passed since I shadowed students around Faircrest High School. The five students in this study have graduated and moved out of town, but most remain in touch with me through periodic phone calls and letters. I decided to write the following few pages as a way to share some of the students' more recent experiences and to satisfy the curiosity of readers who wanted to know more about the lives of the adolescents depicted in the portraits.

Kevin

Kevin described his junior and senior years as "extremely tough." He took mostly honors and advanced placement courses, including AP calculus which nearly "killed" him. He didn't even bother to take the advanced placement test for the course since he was sure he would fail. He was pleased to report that despite his frustrating experiences in some of the more difficult science and math courses, he managed to get his grade point average up to a 3.9. This was a "weighted" GPA, he reminded me, where the University of California system allows students to add points for honors and AP courses. His GPA was helped a bit when he decided to follow his counselor's advice and enroll in Latin I and II, which were considered "easy" compared to the advanced French courses he had planned to take. "I learned my lesson," he said, "no more C's in French for me." He knew he needed better grades to get into a UC school. He also managed to convince the administration to give him "full elective credit" for an A grade he received as an English teaching assistant one semester. Usually teaching assistants are given recognition on their transcripts for their service, but it is rare to receive course credit for their work. "Not bad, huh?" he said, pleased with his powers of persuasion—another way to pad the GPA.

Kevin's hard work at raising his grades eventually paid off when he was accepted to the University of California at Berkeley. When I spoke to him during his freshman year, he seemed to be following his usual way of doing school. He had just pulled several "all-nighters" in a row to prepare for his engineering midterms and told me he "completely screwed up" and was "really worried" about his grades. In the first semester, he did well in his history, political science, and drama courses, but he received a C− in math. When I asked why he had decided to major in engineering, especially given his success in the humanities courses, he explained his father's rationale:

> My dad said to apply to the hardest major at the UC schools because it will look impressive, and it's always easy to get out of engineering schools, but it's not always easy to transfer in—which is probably right, but I am dying here. These [engineer-

ing] classes are really hard for me, and the other stuff [history, political science, etc.] is really easy. I know I'm crazy, but try convincing my father about this. I am stuck in this major, at least for awhile.

In high school, Kevin worked hard to please his father and get accepted to a "good" university. In college, it seems that Kevin is caught once again in a grade trap, where he strives to meet his father's expectations, even if they conflict with his own academic skills and desires.

Kevin's voice brightened when we discussed his PenPals project. He told me that Ian's sister was now in charge and that he planned to go home each summer to help sort clothing and supplies. Last year, he, Ian, and the other volunteers set "an all-time record" for school donations, and Kevin confided that he remains "really, really proud, more than anything [he had] ever done" of the service he performed and the "legacy" he left at Faircrest. This year he volunteered to be the Public Service Director in his college fraternity and was planning to design a service project to fit the diverse needs of the Berkeley community.

Eve

When I called Eve during her senior year of high school, she told me that I was her "first human contact in days." She literally had been studying around the clock for her math exam at a local community college, and aside from food breaks here and there, she had not left her room in three days. She loved the college class, especially the fast pace and challenging assignments, but was worried about taking a three-hour final exam. She decided to use our phone call as a "study break" and spent a half an hour describing her busy schedule over the past semester.

Eve was working hard to keep up an A+ grade in biology and to maintain her straight A average in her other courses. She was excited about her Buddhism project in history class and liked her advanced placement English course but was worried that the teacher was not preparing her well for the AP exam: "We only read two books so far, and I am sure that would be really good for, like, college prep English, but we have to take the AP test, and I really need her to prepare us for it. The other class has read so many more and are better prepared." As with her earlier high school experiences, Eve remained focused on tests, scores, and college admissions above all else. She was still involved in several extracurricular activities, including field hockey, band, hospital volunteering, and student government, and had just accepted a volunteer position as a lab assistant at a Space Research Center for ten hours a week. She wanted to write about the experience in her college application essays. "This year is busier than the last," she explained, "because I have college applications, interviews, and scholarship applications on top of all my regular stuff. I'm back on caffeine [No-Doze and coffee] and eat candy in class to stay awake sometimes because I am so busy and so tired." She was still having stomach problems and had been sick several times "probably due to stress."

A few months later, Eve called and said she was "totally depressed." She had been deferred from Harvard's early acceptance program and now had to complete more than eleven other college applications and scholarship forms. She had stayed up all night filling out the paperwork for Yale and was "shocked" when she typed up her list of school activities:

I actually had to take out a few things that I do so it didn't look so random. I mean I added up all the activities and the hours per week, and it looked like all I ever do is work! It doesn't look like

I have a life. Like, I put down mock trial, and music lessons, and sports, and all my activities, and Chinese School . . . and if you count the homework, I was like, "Oh my god!" no wonder I am so tired all the time. . . . So, I took some [activities] out that didn't seem so crucial, and I think it makes me look more focused this way. . . . It's hard because colleges want you to be well rounded and balanced, and not lacking focus, so I am trying to present myself this way.

While many high school seniors might have struggled to find two or three activities to include on their college applications, Eve worried about which ones to cross off. Ironically, she hoped to appear less busy than she actually was.

Ultimately, Eve was accepted to several Ivy League institutions, and though she and her family were pleased with her success, she was still a bit upset that she had been turned down by Harvard, her first choice school. After much deliberation, she chose to attend Princeton University and sent me a letter the day before school started describing some of her fears about college life:

My mother was dead set against relationships in high school . . . and was fervent about my studies. . . . Now I have a real freedom to choose what I want to focus on in college. . . . I intend to focus on the sciences . . . yet, I don't want to have to sacrifice my social life. What scares me is the fact that I don't want to end up as a housewife like my mother. I know that I love the humanities and were I financially independent and secure for the next 50 years, I would probably major in philosophy or anthropology. However, practicality almost demands for me to study within the realm of science and even focus especially on computer science. I'm not saying that I hate it, but I hate how my options are so limited in reality while theoretically, I should study what "calls to me."

Like Kevin, Eve felt obligated to study the sciences even though she preferred the humanities. Both students felt limited by the expectations of their parents and by the promise of greater financial gain.

In November I received another letter from Eve describing her disappointment with the college experience:

> I love and am a little disappointed by Princeton, myself, and others. . . . I find that many people came here feeling that they have to show that they are better than the next person. There is an extremely competitive pre-med atmosphere in my advanced general chemistry class that I find very disappointing. On the other hand, this is really no different from high school.

In a follow-up phone call she told me that she used to believe college would be different from high school, that she could relax, enjoy herself, learn the way she wanted to, but she realized that it was more of the same. She said it was "even more intense" because she was with the "cream of the crop"—all of whom were really smart and competitive like herself. She was playing the same games at college, this time to get into medical school.

She ended the call by telling me that her body was "really learning how to withstand stress." She had stayed up for three days in a row and was off to read cases for her Juvenile Justice League:

> I am really excited, but I worry that I am starting the stress cycle again. They say that the body has to exist within a certain threshold of stress to perform at optimum level, but can I stand it for another four years?

Teresa

Teresa's family moved out of the school district just before her junior year. She had been accepted into The Community Project (TCP)

and wanted to continue to attend Faircrest High in order to participate in the program. Her dance teacher helped her contact the
school superintendent, and, after two meetings at the district office
and several phone calls, Teresa received permission to stay. Similar
to her meeting with the school principal during her sophomore
year, Teresa was pleased that she had the courage to meet with top
administrators to help achieve her academic goals. Though she
had a forty-minute commute to school in the morning, and had
enough trouble getting to school on time when she lived only a few
miles away, she was convinced she would get a better education in
TCP than at the local school in her new town.

When I spoke with Teresa, she was bubbling with enthusiasm
about her new program. "I am learning so many things; it's so different from last year." She felt "really, really challenged" by the
program:

> I have to do work at home these days, and I have to say to my-
> self, "OK, Teresa, get to work. Go do your work." And it's hard
> because sometimes I don't feel like working and I put it off, but
> I get to decide what I am gonna learn and what books I want to
> read and what I want to study. . . . Like, I have been studying
> books by Latino writers, and I wrote a report on global warm-
> ing and a big report on affirmative action. And then I had to give
> a one hour long lesson on Latino music. It was very scary and I
> was so nervous, but I did it. I think I am a better speaker these
> days; I don't get as scared.

> We learn so many things that you don't realize in the other classes
> at school. Like, we learn things that you just aren't aware of in
> the regular classes—political things, things happening in the
> real world, environmental things that are important. So I love it.

Teresa had the same busy schedule as she had during her sophomore year, with family obligations and dance activities, but she reduced her work hours significantly to spend more time on her studies:

> I only work on the weekends at a gas station and can usually do homework there since it's not too busy. Usually, during the week, I leave my house at 6:30 in the morning and have eight periods with no break [TCP counts as four periods], and I get home at, like, 4:15. Then I have to do homework. I go to sleep at 9:00, though, so I am not so tired all the time. Also, I am not getting as sick as last year, only colds, but not as many as last year.

At the end of her senior year, Teresa and I lost touch with one another. Her family had moved again, and I could not locate a forwarding address or phone number. I heard from the high school that she had been admitted to San Francisco State University and planned to major in social work. I later confirmed this with the registrar's office at the college but could not get any more information. I was pleased to hear that she had found a way to finance her college education and that she was pursuing a career working with people, something I believed she might enjoy.

Michelle

Michelle spent most of her senior year singing, acting, and directing. She performed in more than 40 concerts during the fall semester and directed a one-act play in her advanced acting course. She was busier than she had ever been and had frequent colds and sore throats. She continued to do well in her classes despite her poor health and hectic performance schedule and even took a math honors course and a chemistry class at the community college.

Near the end of her senior year Michelle received "top honors" at the statewide drama competition and won a drama scholarship to a small college in Southern California. Though she was still not sure that she wanted to attend college, and had hoped to take a year or two off to help make her decision, she did not want to lose the money for tuition. In June she opted to accept the scholarship and to major in theater performance. When I last spoke with her, she was enjoying college life and was working toward her degree in drama. She had recently been involved in a production of *Macbeth* that was nominated to participate in a national theater festival, and she was about to leave for London for three weeks on a special theater tour.

Roberto

Roberto had a very successful junior year. He was proud of his high grades and was "setting [his] schedule straight to go to college." He was especially pleased with his improvement in English class:

> In English I have a teacher who really encourages me to re-write the papers, because last year, I never really re-wrote the papers, you know. But he encouraged me and, oh my God, on this one paper I went from a C all the way up to an A. I couldn't believe it; I never got an A on a paper before. So my writing is getting better this year. I get B's and some C's instead of all C's.

He was also quite excited about a new computer program that would help him practice for the SAT exams. He was now "more sure than ever" that he wanted to go to a UC school and was still enrolled in the S.O.S. course to help him reach his goal:

> S.O.S. helps me out right now. . . . I mostly stay home and study and then go to work. But I am only working 20 hours a week these days, and they are treating me right. I am a manager and I work closer to my house—so that's good.

A year later, Berto was still doing well in school. He liked almost all of his classes and received his "highest grades ever." The only course he did not enjoy was statistics I. He originally had hoped to take calculus (an AP course), and believed this would look better on his college transcript, but somehow "the rules changed" and he was placed in a statistics course that had been "under-enrolled." I couldn't help but think that any of the other students in this study would have been able to finesse their way into the course they desired. Once again, Berto's inability to play the system seemed to frustrate him. Even with the help of the S.O.S. class, Roberto still had not acquired the kind of system savvy exhibited by the others in the study.

I later learned that Berto had been accepted to a California State University but that he had decided to join the Army instead of starting college in the fall. Just after his senior year of high school he got married and became the proud father of a baby boy. A few months later he left for a U.S. Army base in Korea where he considered taking some night courses to pursue his degree. When I received a holiday card from him a year later, he wrote that he was "too busy to take classes, but [was] still planning to do it at some point."

Appendix A: General Information about the Students in the Study

	Kevin	Eve	Teresa	Michelle (1st qtr.)	Michelle (2nd qtr.)	Roberto
Grade	10	11	10	11		10
Sex	Male Female	Female	Female		Male	
Ethnicity	Japanese/Caucasian	Chinese	Mexican	Caucasian		Latino
Residence	Faircrest suburbs	Faircrest suburbs	Downtown Faircrest	Downtown Faircrest		Downtown Faircrest
Courses	World Literature Honors	American Literature Honors	Business English	The Community Project	Independent Study	World Literature
	European History AP	U.S. History AP	Business U.S. History	Algebra II	American Literature	Seminar on Studying
	Chemistry	Physics AP	Biology	Acting II	U.S. History	Biology
	Algebra II	Calculus BC AP	Algebra I		Psychology	Algebra II
	French III	Spanish VI AP	Spanish III		Algebra II	Spanish II
	PE	Student Government	Business Computing		Acting II	PE
			Mexican Dance		Advanced Music	Health
"Free periods"	1	1	0	1 (because TCP meets for four periods daily)	1 or 2 a day (because ind. study class does not meet daily)	0
Extra curriculars	Soccer, Rugby, Community Service	Numerous clubs, committees, sports, arts, and service activities	Mexican Student Association	Thespian Club, Concert Choir, Community Service	(same as 1st qtr.)	Peer tutoring
Paid work	None	None	35 hrs./week	None	None	20–30 hrs./week
GPA	3.7	3.97	3.4	4.0	4.0	3.5

Appendix B: Common Student Behavior Exhibited in Pursuit of Success

Category	Behavior	Kevin	Eve	Teresa	Michelle	Roberto
System Savvy	Establish allies/form treaties (with teachers, parents, administrators, peers)	Y	Y	Y	Y	Y
	Cheat (copy work, alter records, "wing it," cut class for extra study time)	Y	Y	Y	N	Y (once)
	"Multi-task"	Y	Y	Y	Y	N
	Complete minimum 2 hrs. homework each night	Y	Y	Y	Y	Y
	"Do the max" (more than required on academic assignments)	N	Y	N	Y	Y
	Enroll in non-traditional course or program (not including honors or AP courses)	N	N	Y	Y	Y
	Become "squeaky wheels" (contest teacher's grade/decision)	Y	Y	Y	Y	N
Tolls of Success	Struggle to fulfill extracurricular or non-school commitments (5 hrs. or more per week)	N	Y	Y	Y	Y
	Experience severe anxiety or breakdowns	Y	Y	Y	Y	Y
	Suffer persistent health or sleep problems	N	Y	Y	Y	N
	Compromise values or ideals	Y	Y	Y	Y	Y

Note: Y = Yes, behavior was exhibited. N = No, behavior was not exhibited.

Notes

PREFACE

1. See, for example, Dornbusch (1989); Feldman and Elliot (1990); Simmons and Blythe (1987); LeCompte and Dworkin (1991); and Phelan, Yu, and Davidson (1994), all of which offer good reviews of adolescent behavioral studies concerning these topics.

2. See, for example, some of the classic school ethnographies such as *The Adolescent Society* (Coleman, 1961); *Culture Against Man* (Henry, 1963); *Inside High School* (Cusick, 1973); *Elmtown's Youth and Elmtown Revisited* (Hollingshead, 1975); and *Learning to Labor* (Willis, 1977). These and other more recent works tend to focus on a wide variety of experiences ranging from how students form and sustain peer groups in school (see, for example, Eckert, 1989; Varenne, 1983), to how students work to attain "identity and selfhood"—to "become somebody" in school (Wexler, 1992), to how students experience and specifically resist the process of social reproduction transmitted via the schools (see, for example, Willis, 1977; MacLeod, 1987), to the causes and consequences of dropout behavior (Fine, 1991; Farrell, 1990), to a focus on

the ethos of community in high school (Chang, 1992). The authors have made conscious decisions to write about non-curricular experiences in school, either because they were more interested in peer groups or social identities or because when they looked closely at adolescent life in schools, they discovered that the students themselves were primarily concerned with non-curricular experiences.

3. A search of the literature since the mid 1980s confirms the paucity of studies that explore curricular experiences through the eyes of the adolescents. Erickson and Shultz (1992) in the *Handbook of Research on Curriculum* write: "In sum, virtually no research has been done that places student experience at the center of attention. We do not see student interests and their known and unknown fears. We do not see the mutual influence of students and teachers or see what the student or the teacher thinks or cares about during the course of that mutual influence. . . . Rarely is the perspective of the student herself explored." (p. 467)

". . . The absence of student experience from current educational discourse seems to be a consequence of systematic silencing of the student voice. Most fundamentally, student experience goes unheard and unseen for what appear to be ideological reasons. The commonsense view of educational practice, of what is most important to pay attention to in and about schools, has left little room indeed for the points of view of the very persons who are the first-level consumers of educational services." (p. 481)

A few notable exceptions, for instance, are Sizer (1984); Roth and Damico (1994); Phelan, Davidson, and Cao (1992); Phelan, Davidson, and Yu (1998); Csikszentmihalyi and Larson (1984); Valenzuela (1999); and Davidson (1996). However, none of these studies specifically asks students to reflect in-depth on their curricular experiences over an extended period of time.

4. According to the Annual Community Report Card, 54 percent of the students describe themselves as Caucasian, 23 percent as Hispanic, 14 percent as Asian, 6 percent as African American, and 4 percent as Filipino. (Numbers do not equal 100 percent due to rounding.) There

are no published statistics on the socioeconomic status of students, though one school official believes parent salaries range from "$15,000 a year to well into the millions," and a district spokesperson notes that approximately 10 percent of Faircrest's students qualify for free lunch programs.

5. I assured the adolescents that the study would focus mainly on their curricular experiences in school, and that I would not inquire about other facets of their lives such as love interests; hobbies and activities not connected to school (including possible illicit behavior); or particular issues with peers, families, or work associates not explicitly related to the courses the students were taking. This is not to say that such matters are unimportant or irrelevant to their lives as students. Much current research on adolescent development asserts the importance of families, peer groups, and community influences on students' academic achievement (for instance, Newmann, 1998; Phelan, Davidson, and Yu, 1998; Feldman and Elliot, 1990). However, examining the students' multiple worlds of family, peers, and community would necessitate a broader focus, more time for data gathering, and a vastly different approach for facilitating reflection among the students in the study.

CHAPTER 1. WELCOME TO FAIRCREST HIGH

1. All names in this study are pseudonyms, and in certain cases, distinguishing characteristics have been altered to protect the anonymity of the students and teachers mentioned herein. Unless otherwise attributed, all words within quotation marks have been taken directly from conversations and interviews with participants. In some cases I re-create quotations from memory when the use of a tape recorder was inappropriate, for instance, in the noisy hallways between class periods.

2. Cited from the school's annual report: Faircrest's dropout rate is .57 percent as opposed to the California statewide rate of 4.9 percent. Class sizes average 29 students, compared to an average of 36 per class statewide. And the school's student-to-counselor ratio is 400 to 1, while in some districts, there may be only one school counselor for an entire

population of 2000 students. Furthermore, "close to 50% of the district's teachers hold masters degrees or doctorates."

3. Research confirms they may be right in this assumption. See, for example, Christopher Jencks (1991) on employment rates for college educated males as compared to those with high school degrees. See also Schneider and Stevenson (1999) and Labaree (1997a) on the projected "underutilization" of college graduates and the consequences of credential inflation due to an increase in the number of students pursuing higher education. A credential from a more prestigious university may lead to higher income and job security than a degree from a college considered to have lower standards for admission or fewer academic resources available to students.

4. Over the years, educational goals in this country have changed. In the early nineteenth century, schools promoted broadly accepted goals of basic literacy, democratic citizenship, and moral development in accordance with the dominant cultural values of the time. In the late nineteenth century, the goal of preparing high school graduates for the world of work gained prominence. In addition to these broad school missions, Americans have also held widely varying expectations for what schools ought to achieve. For instance, school success for some communities means reducing poverty, ending segration, promoting multiculturalism and tolerance; others characterize success as fostering habits of good health, teaching critical thinking skills, or instilling certain character traits such as honesty and generosity. These goals and expectations vary across schools and communities and change over time, often leading to conflicting policies and practices. (Larry Cuban, personal communication).

School reformers have attempted various strategies in order to meet the educational goals of the times. For example, Tyack and Cuban (1995) characterize school policy cycles and trends in the 1950s as focusing on a more academically challenging curriculum with greater emphasis on math, science, and English skills. In the 1960s and early 1970s, as a response to new demands from social activists, the high school curriculum became more heterogeneous, and new courses in ethnic studies, bilingual education, and remediation flourished for a time. In the late 1970s and 1980s policy cycles shifted again to promote a "back to basics" approach to education, eliminating "frills" such as art and ethnic studies in order to focus primarily on core academic subjects.

CHAPTER 2. KEVIN ROMONI

1. This statement seems to stem from his parents' admonitions. According to Kevin's earlier statements, his parents believe that he can do better and that he should try harder. I think Kevin has convinced himself that this is true, that he is not fulfilling his potential, which, of course, is a more acceptable belief than the converse—he is working as hard as he can and he is still not meeting their expectations.

2. Eddie Haskell is a fictional character from the television show *Leave It to Beaver* who often complimented adults to win their favor.

3. See below for a glimpse of Kevin's writing style in an essay written about his family for English class.

4. I was never able to determine the real reason behind his kicking the wall. I am still not sure if it was done out of anger and frustration, or if it was truly accidental. I include it here though because it is so different from his usual behavior, and yet the way he finesses the repairing of the wall is so characteristic.

5. Kevin received a B+ in English as his final semester grade. When he passed the teacher in the hallway the following October, he said half jokingly, "Hey, Mr. K, how does an A− first semester, and a B+ third quarter, and an A− for fourth quarter average out to a B+ for the year?" The teacher said, "It doesn't. I had you down for an A− both semesters." He and Kevin went back to the classroom to check the gradebook, and the teacher changed the grade to an A− "right on the spot." Kevin said, "It was lucky I brought it up because, I mean, I was just going to let it go, but I thought an A− [fourth quarter] shows improvement and usually second semester counts more . . . so I got a 3.7 GPA after all." Though it is unclear whether the teacher made a mistake

on Kevin's report card originally, or, when confronted by Kevin the following semester, he changed his mind, it is evident that Kevin benefited from questioning the mark. In my observations, most students view the report card as final and immutable, and Kevin's action reflects both his high status in the school and his determination to succeed.

6. I am somewhat surprised that he does not mention his success in soccer as a source of great pride. Perhaps Kevin does not discuss this sports activity with me because soccer season ended a few weeks before I began shadowing him, or because he does not consider soccer a type of "work"—the term I used when I asked him the question.

7. He makes a distinction here between "school" project, one which was done specifically for a course, and his community service project that originated from work done in his ninth grade English class, but which is no longer associated with a school course. The Family Portrait is the *school* project of which he is most proud this year, but PenPals (described below) is the "thing" he is most proud of for the year.

8. I include a passage here for reference. Because he read the story aloud to me (on tape), the spelling and grammar presented here may not match the written essay.

CHAPTER 3. EVE LIN

1. Associated Student Body: Eve is an elected member and her sixth period class is devoted entirely to working on ASB administrative projects.

2. I want to clarify that this is Eve's sense of what life is like for a student in the school's college preparatory track (as opposed to the honors track or the general track). Many of the students I observed in the college prep track, including Roberto in Chapter 6, do not lead this "ideal" lifestyle. Eve is, however, most likely correct that most of the college prep students will not be accepted to Ivy League universities.

3. This observation seems significant for many reasons. It shows that Eve's diligence and focus on grades is shared by several other students in this community, and that Eve believes there is a cultural pattern evident in Asian students' success rate.

4. Eve describes many of her "Chinese friends" as good students who do school in the "typical Asian, stressed-out way." Here, she refers to a common stereotype that Asian students, as a group, are more diligent and successful in school—a stereotype perpetuated by the high number of Asian American students in Faircrest's honors and advanced placement courses. Several researchers have studied this Asian American "success story," and have written about its problems, particularly that it fails to account for the immense diversity of Asian American subgroups and that it neglects important differences in socioeconomic status and educational background of family members. Most of the studies I found emphasize the need for further research on the relationship between educational achievement and Asian American subgroup culture, and especially the correlation between parental expectations of success and teenage suicide (see, for example, Walker-Moffat, 1995; Liu, Yu, Chang, and Fernandez, 1990). In any case, Eve believes her motivation and success in school is related to her Chinese upbringing, and she wonders what her experience would be like had she "grown up in a different culture."

5. Oakes (1985) writes about the problems of this type of tracking. The honors class selection process may "protect" students from overextending themselves, but it also effectively perpetuates class and race barriers in the school. Often, the students in the regular courses, many of whom come from lower socioeconomic backgrounds, cannot meet the skills and knowledge requirements to get into the honors classes.

6. This behavior corresponds with Julia Duff's (1997) findings on the peer relationships between economically privileged female adolescents.

7. Eve designed a new activity card for the school. Students use the cards to get into dances and sporting events. Eve came up with the idea to sell advertisements and coupon space on the back to local food and retail stores, so the additional revenue could be used to defray costs of school events.

8. I was not able to observe Eve in Chinese school and rely only upon her self-report here.

CHAPTER 4. TERESA GOMEZ

1. She can fulfill high school graduation requirements and most state college requirements by taking six courses per year (FHS Course Guide, p. iii).

2. For example, as I mention above, she is able to serve as a translator for family members. In addition, she has received several high grades on oral reports in her history class.

3. Students were asked to choose research topics on "American inventions" for the first report and on "conflicts" for the second.

4. Perhaps if she had been given a sense of context for the films or an explanation of events that occurred before and after the war, she might have had a better understanding of this historical period. Some school reform efforts advocate fewer assignments and alternative assessment strategies (see Ted Sizer's Coalition of Essential Schools [Sizer, 1984, 1992], for instance), but in this particular classroom the "less is more theory" did not seem to produce the kind of in-depth knowledge the teacher had hoped for. One reason may be that the students did not feel compelled to "learn" information unless they were to be tested on it.

5. Attending Saturday school is a punishment reserved for students who have accrued four or more unexcused absences or at least twelve unexcused tardies. The students spend most of the day cleaning the school campus and working on their homework assignments. "Getting out of Saturday school" means Teresa's mother writes her a note that serves to excuse the previously unexcused absences.

6. The first time I heard one of Teresa's teachers use the word plagiarism was near the end of the year (May 20). The teacher critiqued a group's history report by saying, "The students did not analyze their audience; they were too general; their report was too long, and they plagiarized—they copied their sources." This was the only mention of the concept I heard during the semester, and based on most of the reports I saw, the majority of the students had not yet learned the proper use of citations. Hence, Teresa's statement seems fairly accurate.

7. Teresa knew I was shadowing a student in The Community Project, which also sparked her interest in the course. I told her a little about

the curriculum, and this prompted her to ask a friend in the program for more details.

8. Though she claims to recognize the false stereotypes that exist about the Business House and Community students, Teresa does not recognize that she may be perpetuating stereotypes about the "white" students. She bases her claims on rumors she hears from her peers—a disproportionate number of white students attend awards night, a disproportionate number are enrolled in honors courses, the "rich" kids' parents will somehow buy their way into college, etc. The school does not keep statistics that would confirm or negate these assumptions, and though my own observations confirm fewer Mexican and African-American students in the honors courses, it is beyond the scope of this study to report on these issues. My point is to note Teresa's feelings of unfair behavior at Faircrest and to convey her view on one reason why the Business House was not as effective as it could have been. For more examples of students' conceptions of race relations and racism at school, see Davidson (1996); Valenzuela (1999); MacLeod (1987); and Peshkin (1991).

CHAPTER 5. MICHELLE SPENCE

1. This quotation and the ones in the following paragraph come from a book Richard wrote on the process of creating and teaching TCP. I cannot cite the actual book title and author's name for reasons of confidentiality.

2. The following information about the meeting comes from Michelle who heard it from Lisa Fogarty. Ms. Fogarty later verified the accuracy of Michelle's statements.

3. Michelle bases her opinion of honors courses on her own experiences and those of some of her friends. I saw a wide range of honors courses over the semester, and though some closely resembled the college preparatory courses with a somewhat faster pace, others struck me as fairly innovative. Some of the honors level courses I observed when shadowing Kevin and Eve, for instance, offered non-traditional assignments such as Eve's NASA project and Kevin's I-search paper,

which at least a few of the students believed were more interesting and challenging than some of their other assignments.

4. Kevin was also in this class, and though the teacher believed he, too, was "a good kid," she did not afford him the same trust. Perhaps this was because he did not consistently receive the high grades Michelle did. One might ask if the students who were not performing as well on tests and homework might not have benefited from the trusting relationship the teacher established with Michelle. See Chapter 7 for more on teacher-student treaties and other success strategies, and see Powell, Farrar, and Cohen (1985) and Sedlack, Wheeler, Pullin, and Cusick (1986) for other sources on classroom treaties and bargains.

5. There are several reasons why Michelle might have been frustrated with this SAT score: In 1995 the SATs were "recentered" to reflect a national average of 500 out of a possible 800 points on each of the two sections of the exam (verbal and math). A combined score of 1200 might have been considered quite high previous to 1995, but the recentering process as well as the growing number of high school graduates (and therefore higher number of students taking the SAT examination) has led to a marked change in average SAT scores at colleges around the country. For instance, *US News and World Report* (February 2001) lists average SAT scores for Ivy League universities to be between 1360 (25th percentile) and 1590 (75th percentile). Average scores for the University of California system range from 1315 for UC Berkeley, 1285 for UCLA, and 1200 each for UC Irvine, UC Davis, and UC Santa Barbara. Ironically Kevin's father demands that Kevin take the SAT exam a second time to reach his goal of 1200, a score that actually ranks below average for his target school of UC Berkeley. (I thank Barbara Melvoin, school counselor at Belmont Hills School in Belmont, Massachusetts, for this information on changes in the SAT scores.)

6. She told me last year she had wanted to write a novel but that her teacher warned her it would not "count for anything."

7. Elliot Eisner (1994a) and others write persuasively about the need for including arts education in schools precisely because they promote thinking and skills not commonly developed in other courses. See also

Wolf (1992) in the *Handbook of Research on Curriculum* for a review of research on art education, and the work of Heath and McLaughlin (1993) on the value of arts programs outside of school.

8. This reaction seems to coincide with what Dewey (1938) calls a sense of disequilibrium, a critical component of an educational experience that leads toward growth.

9. Michelle performed in *Colored Girls* before I began shadowing her, so I cannot relate my own observations of some of the changes she experienced. I did observe her in several other productions, some of which I describe below.

CHAPTER 6. ROBERTO MORALES

1. Roberto often refers to his stepfather as "dad." He never knew his biological father, though he says he wishes he could visit Puerto Rico one day to meet his father's relatives. Roberto's mother moved from Mexico to the United States where she met and married his birth father. Roberto was born in the United States shortly after they divorced. His mother then married his stepfather (also from Mexico) when Roberto was ten.

2. See the chapter on Carla Chavez in Davidson (1996) for another example of a Latino student who is frustrated and feels distanced from her neighborhood peers when she is placed in a separate school track for the college bound.

3. Though Berto is the only one of the five students in this study who utilizes the tutorial center, I notice that the room is often filled with students, especially around midterms and final exams.

4. For more on establishing an ethic of care in the classroom through interpersonal dialogue see Noddings (1992) and Valenzuela (1999).

5. See, for example, Davidson (1996) on what she calls the "information deficit" experienced by children of parents with limited education (p. 103).

6. This engagement with the curriculum resembles Csikszentmihalyi's concept of flow (1993) which I discuss in the following chapter.

CHAPTER 7. THE PREDICAMENT OF "DOING SCHOOL"

1. All five students maintained at least a 3.4 GPA for the semester, and three (Kevin, Eve, and Michelle) achieved averages of 3.7 or higher.

2. Sizer (1984); Noddings (1992); Heath and McLaughlin (1993).

3. One might argue that this behavior, establishing allies at school, may be a result of my sampling process because I asked counselors, teachers, and administrators to suggest students for my study. Obviously the students who were not known to at least one of these sources would not have been listed as possible subjects. While this may be true, every student mentioned the importance of finding a caring adult to help him or her achieve certain privileges, and surely the literature on at-risk students and drop-outs attests to the importance of becoming known at the school in order to avoid falling through the cracks. See, for example, LeCompte and Dworkin (1991) and Horenstein (1993).

4. Many researchers have noted a "mutual dependency" between students, teachers, and school staff, where an adult's commitment to a student heightens possibilities for student achievement, and vice versa, where teachers and students collude to produce student failure. The treaties (Powell, Farrar, and Cohen, 1985) described in Michelle and Teresa's portraits serve as good examples of the dual nature of this student-staff dependency. See, for example, LeCompte and Dworkin (1991) for the phrase "mutual dependency" (p. 179). See also McDermott (1993); Erickson (1984); Sizer (1984); and Sedlack et al. (1986).

5. See for example Christopher Jencks (1991) on employment rates for college educated males as compared to those with high school degrees. See also Schneider and Stevenson (1999) and Labaree (1997a) on the projected "underutilization" of college graduates and the consequences of credential inflation.

6. Griffin (1993); Fine, Mortimer, and Roberts (1990).

7. On a particularly frustrating day, Michelle watched a disturbing excerpt from the movie *Cybil* in her psychology class and a violent montage from the movie *Born on the Fourth of July* in history class. Neither teacher had enough time to help students reflect on the jarring

events depicted in the films, and Michelle (and I) left the classes quite shaken. Five minutes later, she was expected to smile and sing cheerfully in music class as if nothing powerful had just occurred.

8. For good examples of how some "low-achieving" students do high school, see Barbara Porro's "Playing the School System: The Low-Achiever's Game," in Eisner (1994b, pp. 253–272), and several of the portraits in Donmoyer and Kos (1993), particularly Kos' "Nobody Knows My Life But Me!" (pp. 49–78).

9. For more on the educational differences resulting from inequities in cultural, social, and economic capital, see, for instance, MacLeod (1987); Davidson (1996); Valenzuela (1999); and Apple and Weis (1983).

10. Many students are not this hopeful about their futures, as some urban youth face realistic possibilities of early death or continued poverty and see little reason to strive for long-term goals in a system over which they have no control. For more on attitudes of urban youth toward future goals see MacLeod (1987); Brantlinger (1993); McLaughlin, Irby, and Langman (1994); and Nightingale and Wolverton (1993).

11. This observation corresponds in part with the findings of Steinberg (1996). In Steinberg's study, working 20 hours or more per week was found to be harmful to academic achievement because a student had less time to devote to schoolwork and was more likely to suffer from fatigue and to fall asleep during class. Steinberg also found that the majority of students who worked many hours each week "cut corners" by taking easier courses or cheating and that they eventually lost interest in school due to the "excitement of earning large amounts of spending money" (p. 171). Though Berto did not seem at risk of losing interest in school due to his long work hours or increased spending money, he did have to find ways to cut corners in order to maintain his high grades. Berto and Teresa seem to refute Steinberg's data on school achievement of youth who work more than 20 hours per week (since they both maintain high grades), but they both had to find ways to manage the huge drain on their time, often at certain cost to their extracurricular interests and college aspirations.

12. Ted Sizer (1984) writes of similar concerns in the first chapter of his book *Horace's Compromise: The Dilemma of the American High School*. See also Powell, Farrar, and Cohen (1985); Sizer (1996); Eisner (1986); and McLaughlin and Talbert (1993).

13. Tyack and Cuban (1995); Eisner (1994a).

14. Tyack and Hansot (1982).

15. The constraints of the school system faced by the students in this study are not unique to Faircrest. Most of these school factors are discussed in other literature, and I list a few here: See for example, some of the educational psychology literature for studies on motivation and the use of outcome-based assessment (Dweck, 1986; Nicholls, 1989; Kohn, 1999). See Gardner (1983); Noddings (1992); and Newmann et al. (1998) on the limitations of certain curricula to develop multiple competencies in students. See Eisner (1986 and 1994a); Tyack and Cuban (1995); Oakes (1985); and Sizer (1992) on school structures that affect student learning.

16. For more on the achievement ideology and its American nature see for instance, Spindler and Spindler (1990).

17. Cited in Hornblower (1997). David Labaree also describes the pursuit of credentials for status and wealth in his books, *The Making of an American High School* (1988), and *How to Succeed in School Without Really Learning: The Credentials Race in American Education* (1997a). He admits that the middle-class drive for credentials as a means for social mobility is not a new phenomenon. Social reproduction theorists have long documented how classes reproduce themselves via the schools. The theorists highlight the inherent inequality in schools as institutions that privilege certain middle class languages and knowledge forms over those traditionally associated with lower classes, and they reveal the enormous advantages that superior social position and cultural capital impart in shaping educational outcomes. Labaree acknowledges the role of social reproduction theory in his work, but relies more on a "credentialing perspective" to document "the growing domination of the social mobility goal, which has reshaped education into a commodity for the purposes of individual status attainment

and has elevated the pursuit of credentials over the acquisition of knowledge" (1997a, p. 5).

Labaree (1997a, 1997b) and others (e.g., DeVitis and Rich, 1996; Bellah, Madsen, Sullivan, Swidler, and Tipton, 1985) argue that the quest for credentials and wealth has become more extreme over time as "getting ahead and getting an education [have become] inseparable in the minds of most Americans" (Labaree, 1997a, p. i), the result of which is to undercut other historical goals of education such as producing competent citizens and productive workers. In short, the authors assert an American drive for social mobility that inherently conflicts with other American ideals, such as integrity and civic responsibility. Whether or not such a view can be warranted goes well beyond the scope of the study. But I do find it interesting that Jules Henry (1963), writing more than 30 years ago, makes a similar claim that America is a "driven culture"—driven by its "achievement, competitive, profit, and mobility drives" (p. 13), and that these drives conflict with our sense of values such as "love, kindness, . . . frankness, honesty, decency . . ." (p. 14). Values represent ideas about good human relations, for Henry, but they do not have the institutional support that drives do. Drives consume Americans; they help both to promote executives and to lead them to heart attacks.

18. Steinberg (1996) and Dornbusch (1989) write about the benefits to students when parents maintain high expectations with firm enforcement of standards, but they do not discuss the possible negative ramifications of this "authoritative" style, the great pressures students feel as they try not to let their parents down.

19. See Goldman and McDermott (1987) who use this phrase in "The Culture of Competition in American Schools."

20. See Levin (1998) who refutes the notion that high test scores and standards can measure the quality of a student's education and, specifically, the preparedness of students as workers for the labor force.

21. See Bellah, et al. (1985) and Spindler and Spindler (1990) on this illusion of meritocracy.

22. Csikszentmihalyi, Rathunde, and Whalen (1993) found that talented students engage with work when it produces an "optimal experience of flow" where students "are completely involved in something to the point of losing track of time and of being unaware of fatigue and of everything else but the activity itself" (p. 14), similar to when Teresa practices dance and Berto finds the organism under the microscope. Newmann (1996) characterizes moments of engagement, or what he calls "authentic achievement," as those moments that have some value beyond school, that foster intrinsic motivation, and that help children attain competency through the practice of adult tasks and disciplined inquiry, much like the "real" tasks and responsibilities the students describe above. Finally, Dewey (1938) describes educational experiences that lead to growth as relating in some way to both past and future experiences, involving action and reflection, and setting up intense desires and purposes. A student may feel a sense of "disequilibrium" such as Michelle's concern about playing a challenging role or Teresa's struggle with a new dance move, which stimulates a certain desire (to perform well), which leads to an active quest to solve the problem (Teresa takes the music home to practice further), which leads to a momentary sense of "stasis" (she has mastered the steps!) and leaves a residue of something learned (the dance and perhaps lessons on perseverance and problem solving). See also Noddings (1992); Heath and McLaughlin (1993); McLaughlin, Irby, and Langman (1994); along with Sizer (1984), Whelage, Rutter, Smith, Lesko, and Fernandez (1989); and Intrator (1999) on specific ways to foster student engagement.

23. See, for example, Ted Sizer's Coalition for Essential Schools (Sizer, 1984 and 1992), the "Small Schools" project out of Chicago, and those mentioned in Horenstein (1993).

24. A number of charter and magnet schools operate this way as do the Coalition Schools and others mentioned in Dryfoos (1990); Sizer (1992); Meier (1995); Wade (1997); Newmann (1996); and Whelage et al. (1989).

25. See schools described in Oakes, Hunter Quartz, Ryan, and Lipton (2000) and in Horenstein (1993).

26. Meier (1995) writing on Central Park East School in New York.

27. Tyack and Cuban (1995) call these reform efforts that attempt to improve schools from the inside out "a kind of adaptive tinkering that preserves what is valuable and remedies what is not" (p. 136). They praise these efforts and encourage more like them where educators work together with parents and community members to decide collectively on the purposes and goals of high school and to effect positive change at the classroom level.

References

Apple, M. W., and Weis, L. (Eds.). (1983). *Ideology and practice in schooling.* Philadelphia: Temple University Press.

Bellah, R. N., Madsen, R., Sullivan, W. M., Swidler, A., and Tipton, S. M. (1985). *Habits of the heart: Individualism and commitment in American life.* Berkeley: University of California Press.

Bourdieu, P. (1977). *Outline of a theory of practice.* Cambridge: Cambridge University Press.

Brantlinger, E. A. (1993). *The politics of social class in secondary school: Views of affluent and impoverished youth.* New York: Teachers College Press.

Chang, H. (1992). *Adolescent life and ethos: An ethnography of a US high school.* London: Falmer Press.

Coleman, J. (1961). *The adolescent society.* New York: Free Press.

Csikszentmihalyi, M., and Larson, R. (1984). *Being adolescent: Conflict and growth in the teenage years.* New York: Basic Books.

Csikszentmihalyi, M., Rathunde, K., and Whalen, S. (1993). *Talented teenagers: The roots of success and failure.* Cambridge: Cambridge University Press.

Cusick, P. (1973). *Inside high school*. New York: Holt, Rinehart, and Winston.

Davidson, A. L. (1996). *Making and molding identity in schools: Student narratives on race, gender, and academic engagement*. Albany: State University of New York Press.

DeVitis, J., and Rich, J. (1996). *The success ethic, education, and the American dream*. Albany: State University of New York Press.

Dewey, J. (1938). *Experience and education*. New York: Collier Macmillan.

Donmoyer, R., and Kos, L. (Eds.). (1993). *At-risk students: Portraits, policies, programs, and practices*. Albany: State University of New York Press.

Dornbusch, S. M. (1989). The sociology of adolescence. *Annual Review of Sociology, 15:* 233–59.

Dryfoos, J. G. (1990). *Adolescents at risk: Prevalence and prevention*. New York: Oxford University Press.

Duff, J. L. (1996). *The best of friends: Exploring the moral domain of adolescent friendship*. Unpublished doctoral dissertation, Stanford University, Calif.

Dweck, C. (1986). Motivational processes affecting learning. *American Psychologist, 41:* 1040–48.

Eckert, P. (1989). *Jocks and burnouts: Social categories and identity in the high school*. New York: Teachers College Press.

Eisner, E. W. (1986). *What high schools are like: Views from the inside*. A report to the Stanford School of Education, Stanford-in-the-Schools Project: Curriculum Panel Report. Stanford, Calif.: Center for Educational Research at Stanford.

Eisner, E. W. (1994a). *Cognition and curriculum reconsidered*. (2nd ed.). New York: Teachers College Press.

Eisner, E. W. (1994b). *The educational imagination: On the design and evaluation of school programs*. (3rd ed.). New York: Macmillan.

Erickson, F. (1984). School literacy, reasoning and civility: An anthropologist's perspective. *Review of Educational Research, 54,* 525–546.

Erickson, F., and Shultz, J. (1992). Students' experience of the curriculum. In P. Jackson (Ed.), *Handbook of research on curriculum* (pp. 465–485). New York: Macmillan.

Farrell, E. (1990). *Hanging in and dropping out: Voices of at-risk high school students.* New York: Teachers College Press.

Feldman, S. S., and Elliot, S. (Eds.). (1990). *At the threshold: The developing adolescent.* Cambridge, Mass.: Harvard University Press.

Fine, G. A., Mortimer, J. T., and Roberts, D. F. (1990). Leisure, work, and the mass media. In S. S. Feldman and S. Elliot (Eds.), *At the threshold: The developing adolescent* (pp. 225–252). Cambridge, Mass.: Harvard University Press.

Fine, M. (1991). *Framing dropouts.* Albany: State University of New York Press.

Gardner, H. (1983). *Frames of mind: The theory of multiple intelligences.* New York: Basic Books.

Goldman, S. V., and McDermott, R. (1987). The culture of competition in American schools. In G. D. Spindler (Ed.), *Education and cultural process: Anthropological approaches* (pp. 282–299). (2nd. ed.). Prospect Heights, Ill.: Waveland Press.

Griffin, C. (1993). *Representations of youth: The study of youth and adolescence in Britain and America.* Cambridge: Polity Press.

Heath, S. B., and McLaughlin, M. W. (Eds.). (1993). *Identity and inner-city youth.* New York: Teachers College Press.

Henry, J. (1963). *Culture against man.* New York: Vintage Books.

Hollingshead, A. (1975). *Elmtown's youth and Elmtown revisited.* New York: J. Wiley.

Horenstein, M. A. (1993). *Twelve schools that succeed.* Bloomington, Ind.: Phi Delta Kappa Educational Foundation.

Hornblower, M. (1997, February 24). Learning to earn. *Time, 34.*

Intrator, S. (1999). *Spots of time that glow.* Unpublished doctoral dissertation, Stanford University, Calif.

Jackson, P. W. (1968/1990). *Life in classrooms.* (Revised ed.) New York: Teachers College Press.

Jencks, C. (1991). Is the American underclass growing? In C. Jencks and P. Peterson (Eds.), *The urban underclass* (pp. 28–100). Washington D. C.: The Brookings Institution.

Kohn, A. (1999). *The schools our children deserve.* Boston: Houghton Mifflin.

Labaree, D. (1988). *The making of an American high school.* New Haven: Yale University Press.

Labaree, D. (1997a). *How to succeed in school without really learning: The credentials race in American education.* New Haven: Yale University Press.

Labaree, D. (1997b). Public goods, private goods: The American struggle over educational goals. *American Educational Research Journal, 34*(1), 39–81.

LeCompte, M. D., and Dworkin, A. G. (1991). *Giving up on school: Student dropouts and teacher burnouts.* Newbury Park: Corwin Press.

Levin, H. M. (1998). Educational performance standards and the economy. *Educational Researcher, 27*(4), 4–10.

Liu, W. T., Yu, E. S., Chang, C., and Fernandez, M. (1990). The mental health of Asian American teenagers: A research challenge. In A. Stiffman and L. Davis (Eds.), *Ethnic issues in adolescent mental health* (pp. 92–112). Newbury Park: Sage.

MacLeod, J. (1987). *Ain't no makin' it: Leveled aspirations in a low-income neighborhood.* Boulder: Westview Press.

McDermott, R. P. (1993). The acquisition of a child by a learning disability. In S. Chaiklin and J. Lave (Eds.), *Understanding practice* (pp. 269–305). Cambridge: Cambridge University Press.

McLaughlin, M. W., Irby, M. A., and Langman, J. (1994). *Urban sanctuaries.* San Francisco: Jossey-Bass.

McLaughlin, M. W., and Talbert, J. E. (1993). *Contexts that matter for teaching and learning: Strategic opportunities for meeting the nation's education goals.* Stanford, Calif.: Center for Research on the Context of Secondary School Teaching.

Meier, D. (1995). *The power of their ideas: Lessons for America from a small school in Harlem.* Boston: Beacon Press.

Newmann, F. M., and Associates. (1996). *Authentic achievement: Restructuring schools for intellectual quality.* San Francisco: Jossey-Bass.

Newmann, F. M. (1998). How secondary schools contribute to academic success. In K. Borman and B. Schneider (Eds.), *The adolescent years: Social influences and educational challenges* (pp. 88–108). Chicago: University of Chicago Press.

Nicholls, J. G. (1989). *The competitive ethos and democratic education.* Cambridge, Mass.: Harvard University Press.

Nightingale, E. O., and Wolverton, L. (1993). Adolescent rolelessness in modern society. In R. Takanishi (Ed.), *Adolescence in the 1990's* (pp. 14 – 28). New York: Teachers College Press.

Noddings, N. (1992). *The challenge to care in schools.* New York: Teachers College Press.

Oakes, J. (1985). *Keeping track: How schools structure inequality.* New Haven: Yale University Press.

Oakes, J., Hunter Quartz, K., Ryan, S., and Lipton, M. (2000). *Becoming good American schools.* San Francisco: Jossey-Bass.

Peshkin, A. (1991). *The color of strangers, the color of friends.* Chicago: University of Chicago Press.

Phelan, P., Davidson, A. L., and Cao, H. T. (May, 1992). Speaking up: Students' perspectives on school. *Phi Delta Kappan,* 695–704.

Phelan, P., Yu, H. C., and Davidson, A. L. (1994). Navigating the psychosocial pressures of adolescence: The voices and experiences of high school youth. *American Educational Research Journal, 31*(2), 415–447.

Phelan, P., Davidson, A. L., and Yu, H. C. (1998). *Adolescents' worlds: Negotiating family, peers, and school.* New York: Teachers College Press.

Powell, A. G., Farrar, E., and Cohen, D. K. (1985). *The shopping mall high school: Winners and losers in the educational marketplace.* Boston: Houghton Mifflin.

Roth, J., and Damico, S. B. (1994). *Broadening the concept of engagement: Inclusion of perspectives on adolescence.* (ERIC Document Reproduction Service No. ED371004).

Sedlack, M. W., Wheeler, C. W., Pullin, D. C., and Cusick, P. A. (1986). *Selling students short: Classroom bargains and academic reform in the American high school.* New York: Teachers College Press.

Schneider, B., and Stevenson, D. (1999). *The ambitious generation: America's teenagers motivated but directionless.* New Haven: Yale University Press.

Simmons, R. G., and Blythe, D. A. (1987). *Moving into adolescence.* New York: Aldine de Gruyter.

Sizer, T. R. (1984). *Horace's compromise: The dilemma of the American high school*. Boston: Houghton Mifflin.

Sizer, T. R. (1992). *Horace's school: Redesigning the American high school*. Boston: Houghton Mifflin.

Spindler, G., and Spindler, L. (1990). *The American cultural dialogue and its transmissions*. London: Falmer Press.

Steinberg, L. (with Brown, B., Dornbusch, S.). (1996). *Beyond the classroom: Why school reform has failed and what parents need to do*. New York: Simon and Schuster.

Tyack, D., and Cuban, L. (1995). *Tinkering toward utopia: A century of school reform*. Cambridge, Mass.: Harvard University Press.

Tyack, D., and Hansot, E. (1982). *Managers of virtue: public school leadership in America, 1820–1980*. New York: Basic Books.

U.S. News and World Report. (February 2001). http://usnews.com/usnews/edu/college rankings .

Valenzuela, A. (1999). *Subtractive schooling: U.S.-Mexican youth and the politics of caring*. Albany: State University of New York Press.

Varenne, H. (1983). *American school language*. New York: Irvington.

Varenne, H., and McDermott, R. (1998). *Successful failure: The school America builds*. Boulder: Westview Press.

Wade, R. C., (Ed.). (1997). *Community service-learning: A guide to including service in the public school curriculum*. Albany: State University of New York Press.

Walker-Moffat, W. (1995). *The other side of the Asian American success story*. San Francisco: Jossey-Bass.

Wexler, P. (1992). *Becoming somebody: Toward a social psychology of school*. London: Falmer Press.

Whelage, G. G., Rutter, R. A., Smith, G. A., Lesko, N., and Fernandez, R. R. (1989). *Reducing the risk: Schools as communities of support*. London: Falmer Press.

Willis, P. E. (1977). *Learning to labour*. Westmead: Saxon House.

Wolf, D. P. (1992). Becoming knowledge: The evolution of art education curriculum. In P. Jackson (Ed.), *Handbook of research on curriculum* (pp. 945–963). New York: Macmillan.